THE
MIRACLE
CLUB

"The American lineage of mind metaphysics, or positive thinking, takes a beating from both the religious right and the intellectual left, who seem to share in little other than this fear and loathing of the possibility that we might actually be able to imagine ourselves into other realities, histories, and humanities. This same tradition has recently lacked a real intellectual voice willing to answer these too-certain critics and tackle some of the most difficult questions around this astonishing possibility, including the problem of suffering and just how this might all work. Not anymore. Enter Mitch Horowitz. Enter *The Miracle Club*. I wish every leader in the human-potential movement would read this book."

JEFFREY J. KRIPAL, J. NEWTON RAYZOR
PROFESSOR OF RELIGION AT RICE UNIVERSITY

"At a time when quantum physicists dare to say things like, 'Our intentions in the future create the past causes of the present,' a reappraisal of spiritual beliefs (and philosophical theories in general) is clearly in order. It is such a critical assessment that Mitch Horowitz proposes in this book: the values and visions that inspired America assumed that 'greatness' should be measured not only in terms of material riches but of human progress. The lesson is important and timely."

JACQUES VALLÉE, COMPUTER SCIENTIST,
VENTURE CAPITALIST, AND AUTHOR OF *THE EDGE OF REALITY*

"It is rare that I find a book that still strikes me as both fresh and true. Horowitz single-handedly reenergizes the New Thought genre, giving it a much-needed update. *The Miracle Club* moves the reader far beyond the simple promise of wealth and happiness; it moves us to consider what those words actually mean. *The Miracle Club* then gives readers the tools to begin building their lives anew and the wise conviction to create a genuine life which fulfills self-potential and serves others."

REGINA MEREDITH, HOST OF *OPEN MINDS* AND
CREATOR OF REGINAMEREDITH.COM

"As part of my scientific work, I study the relationship between mind and matter under strictly controlled laboratory conditions. I've found that those who laugh the loudest about the 'power of affirmations' will often ask me, but only after drinking a few beers and in hushed tones, 'Seriously, do thoughts really influence reality?' I respond by saying that based on the results of hundreds of published scientific experiments, it appears that yes, they really do. But that's not what they want to know. They're asking if their thoughts affect their reality in their everyday lives. To answer that question, there's only one way to find out—try it yourself. For the clearest and most eminently rational description of exactly how to test the power of your thoughts, there is simply no better choice than Mitch Horowitz's *The Miracle Club*."

DEAN RADIN, PH.D., CHIEF SCIENTIST AT THE
INSTITUTE OF NOETIC SCIENCES AND AUTHOR OF *REAL MAGIC*

"Mitch is a contemporary Diogenes without the cynicism, a Socrates minus the coyness, a Kierkegaard with a happier spirit, an everyman's philosopher who roams freely among the world's great ideas, especially those that have been forgotten, hidden, or otherwise dismissed. The world needs his voice and insights now more than ever."

GREG SALYER, PRESIDENT AND CEO OF THE
UNIVERSITY OF PHILOSOPHICAL RESEARCH

"An erudite and impassioned call for a deeper understanding of the positive-thinking movement. Mitch Horowitz, historian, scholar, and New Thought practitioner, states his case in this beautifully written and eminently practical book. A wonderful read for those familiar with the tenets of New Thought and those who are just embarking on its study and application."

PAUL SELIG, AUTHOR OF *I AM THE WORD: A CHANNELED TEXT*

"Mitch's critical new thinking brings a welcome discipline and honesty to fields too often redolent of fool's gold. One hopes both critics and advocates of New Thought read this book; they need to. But bring a knapsack. There's more than a pocketful of miracles here."

GARY LACHMAN, AUTHOR OF *DARK STAR RISING*

THE MIRACLE CLUB

How Thoughts Become Reality

MITCH HOROWITZ

Inner Traditions
Rochester, Vermont

Inner Traditions
One Park Street
Rochester, Vermont 05767
www.InnerTraditions.com

Text stock is SFI certified

Library of Congress Cataloging-in-Publication Data
Names: Horowitz, Mitch, author.
Title: The miracle club : how thoughts become reality / Mitch Horowitz.
Description: Rochester, Vermont : Inner Traditions, [2018] | Includes
  bibliographical references.
Identifiers: LCCN 2018003884 (print) | LCCN 2018020414 (ebook) |
  ISBN 9781620557662 (pbk.) | ISBN 9781620557679 (ebook)
Subjects: LCSH: New Thought. | Positive psychology. | Attitude (Psychology)
Classification: LCC BF639 .H6833 2018 (print) | LCC BF639 (ebook) |
  DDC 150.19/88—dc23
LC record available at https://lccn.loc.gov/2018003884

Printed and bound in the United States by Lake Book Manufacturing, Inc. The text stock is SFI certified. The Sustainable Forestry Initiative® program promotes sustainable forest management.

10 9 8 7 6 5 4 3 2 1

Text design and layout by Virginia Scott Bowman
This book was typeset in Garamond Premier Pro, Legacy Sans, and Hypatia Sans with New Caledonia and Gill Sans used as display typefaces

To send correspondence to the author of this book, mail a first-class letter to the author c/o Inner Traditions • Bear & Company, One Park Street, Rochester, VT 05767, and we will forward the communication, or contact the author directly at **https://mitchhorowitz.com**.

Metaphysics is dangerous as a single pursuit. We should feel more confidence in the same results from the mouth of a man of the world. The inward analysis must be corrected by rough experience. Metaphysics must be perpetually reinforced by life; must be the observations of a working man of working men; must be biography . . .

RALPH WALDO EMERSON,
POWERS AND LAWS OF THOUGHT

❈

To working people everywhere

In memory of Helen Wilmans

PURPOSE.

Ralph Waldo Emerson called for a "Philosophy for the People"—a simple, dynamic, truthful guide to living ethically and with power. This is my response to that call. My wish is to bring a new tone of maturity to the most popular (and disparaged) of all modern philosophies: positive thinking, or New Thought, which grew partly from Emerson's work and has spread, in various forms and differing vocabularies, throughout modern life. The guiding principle of positive-mind metaphysics is: *thoughts are causative*. I consider this outlook "applied Transcendentalism" and explore it on practical terms in this book.

I call this book *The Miracle Club* in homage to my heroes who run throughout it: men and women of the late nineteenth and early twentieth centuries who blazed a path of practical spirituality for everyday people, and who dedicated years of personal experimentation and search to distilling simple, effective methods by which to expand your day-to-day experience and possibilities. The term "Miracle Club" has its earliest roots in a group of esoteric seekers who banded together in New York City in 1875 to explore the ineffable. That year, one of the club's founders received a mysterious letter telling him: "Don't give up thy club. TRY." This book is, in some regards, a resumption of their efforts. I define miracles, quite simply, as circumstances or events that surpass all conventional or natural expectation. I ask you to join me in pursuing such possibilities in your own life—not only through the medium of ideas, but also in a more direct manner, as I describe at the end of the book.

In laying out these aims, I refuse to shrink from the one question before which every ethical and spiritual philosophy must stand: *Does it work?* Yes, mind metaphysics works. It is a philosophy of results. If you determinedly join my experimentation in this book—and if you follow these ideas and methods as though your life and happiness are at stake (which they may be)—you can evaluate the results in the quality of your daily experience, and in how your conduct affects others. In matters of practical philosophy, experience is the only means of empiricism.

CONTENTS

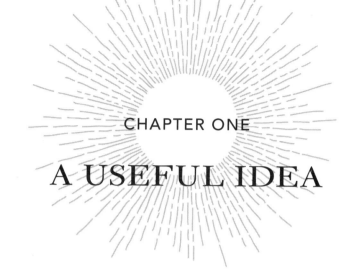

CHAPTER ONE

A USEFUL IDEA

For all the radical changes in how we live over the past 150 years, from the rise and fall of political ideologies to the revolutions in medicine and technology, the basic sense of human identity expressed by Shakespeare remains intact. Each of us "plays his part," living, serving, struggling, until "mere oblivion."

We sometimes bring a ripple of change to our surroundings, coming to a perspective on God or a Higher Power, or attaining a cherished goal, just as we sometimes suffer a life-altering tragedy. But, overall, we remain bound to a familiar pattern.

One modern idea has challenged this template of life. One idea has suggested that we are not "merely players," but also possess a creative agency that can determine and reshape life. This idea helps us view technological, scientific, and social changes not only as revolutions in themselves, but also as expressions of aptitudes and capacities that grow in response to human aspiration. On an intimate level, this idea may save you when you feel that all possibilities are lost. It is this: *thoughts are causative.*

Born loosely from the traditions of New England mental healing and Transcendentalism in the mid-nineteenth century, this philosophy came to be known as "New Thought." I argue in this book that, for all its shortcomings, and for all its being disparaged by critics as a dogma of wishful delusion, New Thought, in its essentials, is true—

1

and can be tested in your experience. This is a book of practical use.

I also argue in this book that New Thought has stagnated. It has not matured since 1910, the year that marked the death of philosopher William James, who took seriously the challenge that thoughts possess formative properties. James wrote about "the religion of healthy mindedness" as a sympathetic investigator and critic. Today, however, New Thought culture, known by the popular terms positive thinking and Law of Attraction, is often unquestioning and childish in its language and temperament. It is unexperimental. In this regard, its critics are right—yet they are not *right enough*. The perspective of the critics requires leavening by experience. But experience will not touch the staunchest among them simply because they avoid participation in ideas. Most psychologists and journalists are trained to see participation as a corrupt and misleading tool of inquiry. (The medical field has proven more open, as will be considered.)

A case in point appears in the career of literary journalist Lewis Lapham, who helped reinforce today's intellectual tendency that practical spiritual ideas are not worth testing. In 1968, Lapham visited northern India to join the Beatles on their sojourn to the ashram of the Maharishi Mahesh Yogi, the founder of Transcendental Meditation (TM). Lapham was a progenitor of the "New Journalism" (not a term he claimed for himself), an approach to reportage intended to include an expressly participatory element. His widely read, two-part article for the *Saturday Evening Post,* "There Once Was a Guru from Rishikesh," was disdainful of the charismatic, bearded guru and his propagation of TM. Yet it never occurred to Lapham to use the easiest and plainest means available to test his instinct that there was something fishy about the robed man selling bliss: namely, sitting his bottom on a cushion and trying the TM technique. If desired, a mantra, the basic tool of TM, is about as easily attained as a learner's permit to drive—and was at that particular time and place much easier.

In 2017, nearly fifty years after his visit, I asked Lapham, a gentlemanly and approachable man, whether he had learned to meditate at

Rishikesh or another time. His reply: "Even in Rishikesh I didn't practice Transcendental Meditation. The Maharishi furnished me with a mantra, but I failed to employ it as a stairway to the stars." There was no curiosity to approach the thing being judged.

Cultural journalist Tom Wolfe demonstrated a similarly laissez-faire attitude toward the spiritual trends he covered. Wolfe has privately expressed sympathies for New Age or therapeutic spirituality; but he avoided participation in any of the Aquarian Age spiritual pursuits that he chronicled in the late 1960s and early '70s. Wolfe feared that association with things like Zen, yoga, or TM would make him seem unserious in lettered circles. Again, experience as a means of inquiry was eschewed.

This book is not about arguing for or against a certain style of reportage or social commentary. Rather, it is about the need for *participation* in ethical and spiritual ideas. Readers who want a fuller analysis and history of positive-mind philosophy can find it in my earlier work, *One Simple Idea*. This book is different: it is a guide to use.

I wrote above that the most radical idea of modern life is that *thoughts are causative*. And that is a fact. This outlook is spiritual or nonphysical in nature, although there are secular variants of it. As you can gather from what I've written, I do not simply view this idea from behind a glass case—I also share it. I have sat through many meetings with producers, reporters, interviewers, and scholars of religion where the conversation invariably turns to the question: "You don't believe this stuff, do you?" Yes, I do believe this stuff. I believe, as did the pioneers of New Thought, that there is a slender thread of difference between mental and metaphysical experience. By metaphysical, I mean the existence of extraphysical influences that accompany and complement cognitive and motor acts. I believe that thinking, in a directed, highly focused, and emotively charged manner, expands our capacity to perceive and concretize events, and relates us to a nontactile field of existence that surpasses ordinarily perceived boundaries of time and thought. This outlook is less a personal doctrine than a line of experimentation. I ask you to join me in these experiments. Our experimentation culminates in the closing chapter, where I venture a theory of what is actually and mechanically occurring when we attempt to use the formative agencies of thought.

Let me emphasize: If I posit a connection between the individual and some kind of higher capacity of the mind, that does not mean that only "one thing"—a law of mentation—is going on in your life. Lots of events, whether biological, mechanical, or metaphysical, can be simultaneously occurring. We live under many laws and forces, of which the impact of the mind is one. For example, compare the mind to gravity. The law of gravity is ever operative, but it is mitigated by other laws, such as mass. The experience of gravity radically differs on the moon, Earth, and Jupiter. So it is with the mind: surrounding events and realities matter.

What's more, one event may be symptomatic of another. Some science journalists, for example, argue that the release of pain-reducing endorphins is "what happens" during the placebo response. Yet many things occur during the period of hopeful expectancy that sometimes precedes physical relief. The production of antibodies, combatting of pathogens, strengthening of immunity, and reductions in inflammation are among the more measurable. It could also be argued that these and other physical events, when following periods of intensive prayer, meditation, or improvements in morale, are what mental healing and the spiritual appeal *look like* in the body.

The question of "what happens" is equally intriguing in matters of psychological health. Many psychiatrists have noted that the expectation of recovery from depression is the key factor in whether any recovery occurs at all. I have witnessed psychological and emotional recovery beginning when an individual makes a commitment to undergo a serious form of treatment, such as electroshock therapy or hospitalization— relief begins to arrive *before* the treatment actually starts. I personally know of cases where the treatment itself became unnecessary, or was more efficacious than expected, because improvement was in process following the patient's commitment and *before* the start date. Therapists have observed that the commitment itself, and the willingness it represents to charge at a problem with all available resources, is therapeutically meaningful. The sense of moral agency that arises when you cross a threshold, when you commit to withholding nothing in pursuit of a solution, can amount to the solution that is sought. The mental act is catalyzing.

I want this book to be useful, and there are, of course, many good and practical guidebooks to New Thought. Why add another? Because, as alluded to earlier, New Thought has not grown. Or rather its temperament and discrimination have not. Its ideas appear in many potent works from *The Science of Mind* by Ernest Holmes to *Think and Grow Rich* by Napoleon Hill to *Resurrection* by Neville Goddard (my personal favorite). Recent books by figures like Deepak Chopra and Gregg Braden have connected New Thought to developments in quantum theory. But the philosophy has fled from rather than embraced its toughest questions, namely: the persistence of catastrophe, the inevitability of physical decline, and episodes of failure and illness even in atmospheres where hope, resilience, and morale prevail. Above all, New Thought has failed to develop a theology of suffering. It has failed to take seriously gaps and inconsistencies in its ideas—often explaining exceptions to its worldview by resorting to jerry-rigged versions of karma, or claims that a single thought from millennia ago can affect someone today, which amounts to little more than an admission of the very randomness of life that the philosophy seeks to reject.

At the lowest end of the scale, some New Thought enthusiasts still resort to a victim-blaming card, claiming, covertly or blatantly, that someone who is sick or has suffered catastrophe wasn't being "just right" with his or her thought vibes or affirmative prayers. New Thoughters hate being reminded they do this; but I've seen it.

It must also be said that New Thought culture, for all its truths and wide-ranging influence on modern life (often under different names and without recognition of the original source), can demonstrate a decided childishness. Services at many New Thought–oriented churches are a cross between pep rallies and preschool birthday parties, with attendant exhortations from the pulpit: "Isn't this the most fun ever?" Slogans come cheap and fast: "Pessimists need a kick in the cant's." Many New Thought writers, with a few serious exceptions like Harvey Bishop and David Spangler, are willfully ignorant of political, religious, and social history, proffering an ahistorical and socially irrelevant tone.

As a longtime publisher and writer within the metaphysical culture, I am often asked: "What current books or writers in New Thought or the positive-mind field excite you?" The answer: Very few. I am unimpressed with the standards of many current authors in metaphysics and spiritual self-help. I know firsthand of numerous cases where authors have created "composite" characters, which is a lame way of incorporating events from several people's lives into one person, artificially heightening a sense of synchronicity and drama. I have seen authors compress or rearrange timelines, less with the aim of graceful storytelling than with inflating a set of events, giving the misimpression that things unfolded more quickly or symmetrically than they really did, or happened in a different order (suggesting, for instance, the absence of recidivism in addiction recovery). Finally, many authors alter names and locales, ostensibly to "protect" someone's privacy, but in reality to protect themselves from scrutiny or verification of their stories.

The methods I've been describing were popularized in 1977 in mystery writer Scott Turow's memoir of his first year at Harvard Law School, *One L.* To his credit, Turow used these devices transparently and purposefully. Readers thrilled at trying to guess who he was talking about. His approach suited a certain endeavor written for a certain purpose. It was never intended, and should not be adopted, as a general method of nonfiction or spiritual storytelling. It has been abused within my field in particular.

Surveying popular spiritual literature, a shrewd reader-reviewer on Amazon once challenged: Where are the "miracles" today that seemed to abound in older New Thought books? Where are the little old ladies from Dubuque, Iowa, who wrote to authors, like Joseph Murphy, author of the 1963 bestseller *The Power of Your Subconscious Mind,* exclaiming their stellar success at using one of his get-rich principles? The truth is, I'm not sure where those stories are. Murphy and others might have benefited from a predigital culture where it was more difficult to scrutinize claims, to retrace footprints and correspondence, and when it was easier, frankly, for writers to make things up.

The respected Protestant minister Arthur Caliandro, the direct successor to the Rev. Norman Vincent Peale at Manhattan's Marble Collegiate Church, acknowledged to me, unprompted, that Peale, author of *The Power of Positive Thinking,* sometimes "juiced up" his stories and sermons. Those of us in the positive-mind culture must face up to those claims. Later in this book, in fact, I reproduce and respond to one of several candid letters written to Joseph Murphy after the author's death, in which dismayed readers asked why his get-rich, get-well methods didn't work wonders for them.

I want to be transparent about the lesser side of our history. None of this, however, is cause for dejection or contention. Despite the shortcomings, and the forays into exaggerated or mawkish claims, modern mind-power methods *have validity.* William James spent the final years of his life, not exclusively but in part, studying and attempting methods in New Thought and related philosophies. He took this outlook seriously. So do I. There is truth to it, and together we will resume the tone and maturity of James's search. We will begin to probe anew. To start with, I promise you this: Nothing in this book is juiced up, diced up, exaggerated, or concealed behind devices.

Let me add a final word about language. Some colleagues have cautioned me that terms like *positive thinking* seem old-fashioned and musty; the phrase puts off younger or more sophisticated readers. There is truth to that. But the "power of positive thinking," to use the title phrase of Peale's 1952 book, has so fully entered the public mind that most people have an immediate association with it. It is plain. For that reason I have continued to use Peale's phraseology, musty or not.

If I, or someone else, came up with something clearer and fresher, I would embrace it. I used the term *applied Transcendentalism* in my prefatory note, but I doubt my Aunt Lois will ever be sold on it. I am also wary of jettisoning old terms, such as ESP, New Age, and occult, simply because they have taken on critical baggage, and one hopes to arrive at something more "respectable." All of the aforementioned terms possess historical integrity and cultural clarity. Hence, I will not be deterred by terminology when exploring why positive thinking, far from belonging to an outdated yesterday, may yet prove the most radical and useful idea of today.

CHAPTER TWO

POWER TO THE PEOPLE

My philosophical hero is Neville Goddard, an English, Barbados-born New Thought teacher, who wrote under his first name. He heard the following words in the midst of a personal vision: "Down with the blue bloods!" To Neville, who died in 1972, privilege did not belong to the rich but to the truly imaginative.

Because of Neville's English background and elegant bearing, many people assumed he was born wealthy. He was not—far from it. Likewise, because of my New York background and surname, many people judged the same of me growing up. A school bus driver upon hearing that I lived in a suburban development with gaudily named streets like Royal Way and Regents Lane said, "Oh, a rich kid, huh?" A truculent writer with whom I worked once (just once) called me "college boy," inferring the same thing.

Here's the truth, of which I rarely speak: My father was a Legal Aid Society attorney in New York City who defended the poorest of the poor. For reasons beyond his control, he lost his job and profession, leaving us to consider applying for food stamps and warming our always-unaffordable home with kerosene heaters. We wore used clothes and scraped together change and coupons to pay grocery bills. There were no Hanukkah, Christmas, or birthday gifts. My sister and I would

9

buy them with our own money, earned from odd jobs, and pretend to friends that they came from our parents. In the words of The Notorious B.I.G., "Birthdays was the worst days."

One night, in desperation, my father stole my mother's engagement ring to pay debts, over which he may have been physically threatened. (He had started carrying mace spray.) They divorced. My older sister and I got by through after-school jobs, student loans, and the precious availability of health benefits through my mother's labor union, the 1199 hospital workers. Given the economic devastation visited on many American homes, including during the still-unhealed 2008 recession, I do not consider our story exceptional.

But when someone assumed then, or does today, that the son of a Jewish lawyer is necessarily born on easy street, he is wrong. This brings me to something else that I rarely mention: Today I am a millionaire. It's not because I'm a hotshot media figure or dealmaker. In my day job, at the time of this writing, I publish occult and New Age books—not your typical path to wealth. My wife, the daughter of a single-mother family, is a television news producer. We raise two sons in Manhattan. We have no family cash cow. And yet, to draw again on The Notorious B.I.G.: "Now we sip champagne when we thirsty." Why is that?

Because Neville, in my estimation, was correct. Wealth, to some extent, comes from within. Let me quote the woman I honor in the dedication of this book, Helen Wilmans. A suffragist and New Thoughter, Wilmans rose from dirt poverty on a Northern California farm in the late 1890s to command a small publishing empire.

"What!" Wilmans wrote in her 1899 book *The Conquest of Poverty*. "Can a person by holding certain thoughts create wealth? Yes, he can. A man by holding certain thoughts—if he knows the Law that relates effect and cause on the mental plane—can actually create wealth by the character of thoughts he entertains." But, she added, such thought "must be supplemented by courageous action." Never omit that.

Wilmans's career was a New Thought parable of liberation. While working as a newspaper reporter in Chicago in the early 1880s, she became one of the pioneering female reporters of that era. Everything had gone against her in life. She was fired from jobs, divorced from her farmer husband, left to raise two daughters on her own, and lived one step ahead of eviction from her Chicago boarding house. More than anything, Wilmans yearned to start her own labor newspaper. She wanted to bring the ideas of mind-power to working people. One day in 1882, she asked her Chicago editor if he would invest in her venture. He dismissed the idea out of hand. In despair Wilmans ran from the newspaper offices (probably not wanting her male bosses to see her in tears) and wandered the darkening streets of Chicago on a November afternoon. She thought to herself: *I am completely alone; there is no one on whom I can depend.* But as those words sounded in her head, she was filled with a sense of confidence. It occurred to her that she did not *have* to depend on anyone else—she could depend on the power of her mind. This was the New Thought gospel.

"I walked those icy streets like a school boy just released from restraint," Wilmans wrote. "My years fell from me as completely as if death turned my spirit loose in Paradise."

Like Wilmans, I had never dreamed of wealth or wanted to be surrounded by fancy things. I believe in labor unions, moderately redistributive tax policies, and personal thrift—not gross consumption. But there is something vitally important to earning a good living, and that fact cannot be hidden or ignored. Nor can this: *Your mind is a creative agency, and the thoughts with which you impress it contribute to the actualized events of your existence—including money.* This statement is absolutely true and should never be neglected. I have tested and verified it within the laboratory of my existence, and I am writing these words at age fifty. I will consider later why it is true, but for now, if you want money, I ask you to wholly embrace it as true. This necessary act of conviction will not, in any case, lead you to rash behavior. It does not suggest neglecting daily obligations or loosening your hands on the plow of effort.

To have wealth you must first want wealth. Do you? Or do you consider money gauche or unimportant? Whether you are an artist or activist, soldier or craftsman, you must see wealth as a necessary and vital facet of your life. You can do far more good with money than without. You must recognize money as a healthful part of existence. Nothing is more duplicitous than someone who runs down acquisitiveness while enjoying money that comes from well-off parents, a situation typical of many in the New York media world in which I work. Or, a public persona who scoffs outwardly at money while employing sticky-fingered lawyers, agents, or other parties to comb the earth for money for them. As a publisher I've seen it many times. By contrast, strong people admit that they *want* money, among other goals, and in so doing are neither in the service of falsehood nor shame.

The same holds true of your ambitions in the world. Spiritually minded people, and all others, should honor their ambitions and pursue them openly and transparently, with due respect to colleagues and competitors. Yet this is frowned upon in many reaches of the contemporary alternative spiritual and New Age cultures. Within these worlds, we recycle ideas from the Vedic and Buddhist traditions and use them to prop up unexamined ideas about the need for nonattachment, transcendence of the material, and the value of unseen things. Writers who can't decipher a word of Sanskrit, Tibetan, or ancient Japanese—the languages that have conveyed these ideas from within the sacred traditions—rely upon a chain of secondary sources, often many times removed from their inception, to echo concepts like nonattachment and nonidentification. We are told that the ego-self grasps at illusions and fleeting pleasures, formulating a false sense of identity around desires, ambitions, attachments, and the need for security. I question whether this interpretation is accurate. In recently working with the Shanghai-based translator of a Chinese publication of my *One Simple Idea,* I found, to my chagrin and bemusement, that Buddhist concepts I thought that I, as a Westerner, had understood were, in my retelling, completely alien to her experience as someone raised within non-Western religious structures.

Our popularized notions of the Eastern theology of nonattachment are cherry-picked from religious structures that were, in their originating cultures, highly stratified and hierarchical. Hinduism and Buddhism, moreover, addressed the lives of ancient people for whom distinctions of caste, class, and status were largely predetermined, and who would have regarded cultural mobility almost as unlikely as space travel. There were social as well as spiritual reasons why worldly transcendence beckoned. Shorn of their cultural origins, concepts of nonattachment today sound tidy and persuasive to Westerners who understandably want something more than the race to the top. (Or, just as often, who fear they may not reach the top and thus desire an alternate set of values.) But this transplanted outlook is often ill fitting and brings no more lasting satisfaction to the modern Westerner than so-called ego gratifications. This kind of ersatz "Easternism" has been with us for several decades, most recently popularized by writers such as Eckhart Tolle and Michael A. Singer, yet it has not provided Westerners with a satisfying response to materialism because it often seeks to divert the individual from the very direction in which he may find meaning, which is toward the compass point of achievement.

Some of my spiritual friends and colleagues have told me that I am too outwardly focused. Isn't the true path, they ask, marked by a sense of detachment from the outer? Doesn't awareness come from within? Isn't there, finally, a Higher Self or essence from which we can more authentically live, rather than succumb to the illusory goals of the lower self or ego, which directs us toward career, trinkets, and pleasure?

I have been on the spiritual path for many years. I have sought understanding within both mainstream and esoteric movements. My conviction is that the true nature of life is to *be generative*. I believe that in order to be happy, human beings must exercise their fullest range of abilities—including the exertions of outer achievement.

Seekers too often divide, and implicitly condemn and confuse, their efforts by relying on terms like *ego* and *essence,* as though one is good and other bad (while neither actually exists beyond the conceptual.) A teacher of mine once joked: "If we like something in ourselves, then we say it comes from essence; if we dislike it, we say it comes from ego." I contend that these and related concepts, like attachment/nonattachment and identification/nonidentification, fail to address the needs, psychology, and experience of the contemporary Western seeker. And, in fact, such concepts do not necessarily reflect the outlook of some of the most dynamic recent thinkers from the Vedic tradition, including the Maharishi Mahesh Yogi (1918–2008) and Jiddu Krishnamurti (1895–1986).

Let me be clear: The inner search and the search for self-expression are matters of extraordinary importance—and extraordinary mystery. I believe that the simplest and most resounding truth on the question of the inner life and attainment appears in the dictum of Christ: "Render unto Caesar what is Caesar's and render unto God what is God's." We are products of both worlds: the seen and the unseen. There is no reason to suppose that our efforts or energies are better dedicated to one or the other. Both exist. Both have veritable claims on us.

I do not view nonattachment as a workable goal for those of us raised in the West, and elsewhere, today. Rather, I believe that the ethical pursuit of achievement holds greater depth, and summons more from within our inner natures, than we may realize. "Satisfaction with our lot," Emerson wrote in his journals on July 28, 1826, "is not consistent with the intentions of God & with our nature. It is our nature to aim at change, at improvement, at perfection."

I recently read a book that I recalled my mother borrowing from our local library when I was eight or nine years old: *Yes I Can,* the autobiography of entertainer Sammy Davis, Jr., published in 1965, the year of my birth. In the public mind, Davis is remembered as a flashy, somewhat self-parodying Vegas performer—but decades before his tuxedoed stage shows, Davis was an innovative prodigy, raised on the vaudeville circuit, where he was subjected to the brutality, insults, and physical assaults that often characterized black life under Jim Crow. These threats followed him into the army during World War II, where he used his skills as an entertainer to mitigate some of the racism around him—though indignities and violence always snared him at unexpected moments. When Davis left the military, he made an inner vow that shaped the rest of his life:

> I'd learned a lot in the army and I knew that above all things in the world I had to become so big, so strong, so important, that those people and their hatred could never touch me. My talent was the only thing that made me a little different from everybody else, and it was all that I could hope would shield me *because* I was different.
>
> I'd weighed it all, over and over again: What have I got? No looks, no money, no education. Just talent. Where do I want to go? I want to be treated well. I want people to like me, and to be decent to me. How do I get there? There's only one way I can do it with what I have to work with. I've got to be a star! I have to be a star like another man has to breathe.

I challenge anyone to question the drive, purpose, and canniness of Davis's words—not to challenge them from a meditation cushion or living room sofa, but from within the onrush of lived experience. Davis was viewing his life from a pinnacle of clarity. Would his worldly attachments and aspirations cause him pain? He was already in pain. At the very least they would relieve certain financial and social burdens— and probably something more. Would his attainment of fame ease his inner anguish? I think he owed it to his existence, as you do to yours, to find out. Whatever your goal may be, you cannot renounce what you haven't attained. So to conclude that success, in whatever form, is not meaningful is just conjecture without first verifying it.

Do not be afraid of your aims, or slice and dice them with melancholic pondering. Find them—and act on them. By living as a productive being, in the fullest sense, you honor the nature of your existence and perform acts of generativity toward others. If you are able, you may then determine from the vantage point of experience and attainment whether your aim responded to an inner need of profound meaning. I won't tell you what you'll find—you may differ from me; I will tell you that this been the case for me.

I wrote earlier that I feel confident in the existence of an extraphysical dimension of life. Following from that, I also assume there is some form of nonphysical or after-death survival. But I do not *know* that. I do know that we have verifiable experiences in *this* world. Jesus didn't say to avert your eyes from the world but to "render under Caesar"; that is, to fulfill both transcendent ethics and worldly requirements. "To be in the world but not of it"—to locate your values on the highest scale, but to dig your well where you stand.

The greatest of worldly requirements, as I'm sure you implicitly feel whether you accept or resist it, is the fulfillment of your self-potential, which includes your command of resources and your ability to influence others through your artistic, commercial, or social activities. Whatever your aim in life, it must be acknowledged that money is necessary. Without it you can do nothing—you will be forced to spend all your time and attention getting it, while anxiously yearning to enact your plans in the world. So, I offer no false demureness on matters of wealth.

If you can agree that money is important, there are two vital, inner steps to opening yourself to money. I purposely offer these steps early in this book because I am unashamed of them, and because I promised you a philosophy of results. Keeping one's word is the cornerstone of the search for meaning.

1. You must possess and pursue a clear and definite aim in life.

By this I do not mean a flimsy, general, or vague desire, and certainly not a set of aims that may be in contradiction (for example, wanting to raise a young family while also wanting to frequently travel). You must know exactly what you want to accomplish, and you must feel it passionately, even obsessively. You must be willing to turn aside everything and everyone who doesn't contribute to your realization of that aim. (I do not necessarily mean family members or people in need.) If that strikes you as ruthless or extreme, it is because you do not yet possess, or are not yet honest about, your definite aim. When you find it, it will be like finding breath itself.

You've heard the expression "no one on his deathbed ever wished he had spent more time at the office." Well, I doubt that principle is true. Pursuing a deeply felt aim is, in fact, rarely a source of regret. The important thing is to be unembarrassed and uncompromisingly honest with yourself about what your central aim is. And remember: it's *yours*—you don't have to advertise it to skeptical friends or family members. It's better not to. Most people are creatures of jealousy. They often run down other people's legitimate aims. Don't invite purposeless scrutiny. Share your ideas only as necessary. Devising a chief aim is so crucial—and so foundational to everything in this book—that I return to it in almost every chapter.

2. You must write down a certain amount of money that you want to make by a certain date in connection with your aim—and be deadly serious about it.

What do you want to earn from the pursuit and realization of your aim? Write it down. Be precise. Set a dollar amount and a date. This is a step that I long resisted. I wanted general prosperity, but eschewed listing some fixed sum. It struck me as narrow. It seemed to violate my sense of ethics and spiritual ideals. I was wrong. I currently have a yellow sticky note pasted inside the back cover of my personal copy of Napoleon Hill's *Think and Grow Rich* (whose jacket and spine I have covered in clear packing tape to keep the book from falling apart after multiple readings). My yellow note is dated 11/23/14 and lists a specific dollar amount, to which I committed to earning by the following year on 11/23/15 (which also happens to be my birthday). I later wrote an addendum on this piece of paper: "This happened!! 5/27/16." The latter date is when I had noticed, entirely by surprise, that the sum I had written down arrived within the given time frame. In the period since I wrote that sum, I have listed another sum yet further off in the future.

As I am writing these words, certain unforeseeable forms of income have flowed to me in considerable amounts, and I've turned away other offers for reasons of preference and time management.

Why does the listing of a sum and date make any difference? Well, it's far more than just jotting down a number and date. You must have that sum and deadline firmly in mind and fully embrace them as goals. It makes you honest and focused about what you desire. The sum should be believably attainable to you. It must be inwardly persuasive. There are always opportunities to go further—but be reasonable at first so that you do not pit the faculties of logic in opposition to your goal. Your mental and emotional aptitudes—innovation, empathy, logic, instinct, and, I believe, some form of extraphysical understanding and communication—will collude in the most sensible and direct way to set you toward your financial goal. You cannot foresee exactly how your aim will come to pass: if you are committed and ethically clear, ever conscious of the financial direction in which you wish to move, possessed of and active toward your plans, and mindful of and obedient to basic religious ethics of plain dealing and honest delivery of your service or product—i.e., something that benefits the user and creates a widening circle of generativity—the means will unfold. Indeed, what we see and experience as a logical progression of events may be accompanied or driven by a higher creative agency, which works in concert with our focused, clarified ideals in the same way that the spiritual appeal and hopeful energies are measurable in certain ways in the body, but are not themselves what *is* measured. In any case, if you recede into laziness, procrastination, dishonesty, exaggeration, or entitlement, the circle of productivity will correspondingly recede and so will the flow of finances to you. (And note that the things I've just mentioned are usually forms of fear.)

Being generative means providing a concrete service, not just expecting payouts from the world in the forms of remuneration, applause, contracts, and open doors. Are you offering a service—or just placing demands on others? Cornering people to read your novel is *not* offering a service. Do you possess, or are you willing to attain, the necessary skills to earn money through whatever career, service, or product you have dedicated yourself to? This consideration is vital because you cannot serve the productivity and betterment of others—and, hence, make financial claims on them—without being able to plant and harvest. Don't dream of being a farmer but *be* a farmer by harvesting a crop and thus having something viable to offer. By your fruits your benefactors will know you.

Some New Thought authors have taken a "fairy dust" approach to riches, promising their readers that visualization and affirmation open up the storehouses of heaven. I recently discovered a cache of letters that readers had sent to the publisher of New Thought pioneer Joseph Murphy more than a decade after the writer and minister's death in 1981. It was heartbreaking to read the yearning, disappointed questions of these earnest correspondents—many of whom were trying to mani-fest money—written to a man now deceased.

I selected one letter below, handwritten by a woman in Tampa, Florida, that typified the needs of many who wrote Murphy. Following her letter, I include what I would say to this woman if I could reach back in time and respond:

August 12, 1993

Dear Dr. Murphy,

I keep reading your book Your Infinite Power to Be Rich *so much that it is falling apart and I still haven't reached my goal of receiving abundance.*

I feel that I must be doing something wrong so that I can't break this poverty syndrome. I keep saying these wonderful affirmations but I think I neutralize them because I don't believe I deserve wealth of any kind.

I would like to be financially secure so that I never have to worry about money again. I would like good, supportive relationships and a soul mate.

Somehow I got the impression from my youth that I didn't deserve anything because I'm no good.

Please help me to get out of my poverty.

Sincerely, _____

Dear _____,

First of all I want to assure you of something—and I want you to remember this for the rest of your life: You are not only good—you are exceptional. You are a leader among people and are part of the nobles of the human race. This is for the simple fact that you have taken steps that so few people ever consider: striving to heighten your place in life, engaging in inner development, and caring enough about such things to take the time to write a letter to an author whose work touched you. Most people never write one letter in their lives. Most never read a single book, or attend a single lecture, with the aim of raising their sense of self-potential. So, please, let us lay that childhood myth immediately to rest. You are exceptional—and this is a fact.

I love Joseph Murphy's work; but I believe that sometimes saying an affirmation—even with depth of feeling—is not enough. The most remarkable people in history, from Joan of Arc to Mahatma Gandhi, led lives of devotion and action. They were ardently committed to affecting things in the world. Whatever your employment, throw yourself into it with passion. Be aware of everything that you can do for your bosses, coworkers, and customers. Be the problem-solver to whom others look for help and advisement. Know more about your job than everyone else, not in a know-it-all way but with the aim of providing service and doing your personal best. Expect—and respectfully require—good wages for your good work. Join a union if you are able and support activists and leaders who defend the rights of workers. But, above all, be the person upon whom all others rely.

Author James Allen was a working-class Englishman who rose from a childhood of poverty to a writing career, largely through his dignity of character and his dogged and intelligent persistence. [We explore his life in a later chapter.] I urge you to read his As a Man Thinketh. *And when you do, remember that his words and ideas weren't the work of someone famous or wealthy. They came from a workingman who had tested them in the laboratory of his own life. Also please read Napoleon Hill's* Think and Grow Rich, *which is useful because it combines a program of mental metaphysics with a plan of action.*

As for good relationships and finding a soul mate, those, too, are noble and right yearnings. My counsel is to associate only with people who are supportive and respectful of your search for self-betterment and spiritual awareness. Seek out those who are engaged, in whatever way, in bettering themselves. Spend no time—or as little time as practicality allows— among cynics, bullies, or unproductive people. Avoid those who gossip, and refuse to listen to rumors or hearsay. (Nothing is more deleterious of our relationships or sense of self-respect than engaging in gossip.) Do this, and you will naturally come into the company of true friends and, hopefully, a soul mate.

I enter into a few moments of prayer every day at 3 p.m. EST—and I would be privileged if you would join me. I wish you every good thing.

Your friend,
Mitch

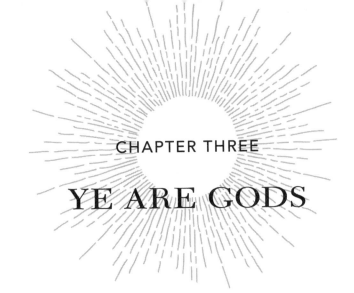

CHAPTER THREE

YE ARE GODS

Transcendentalist philosopher Ralph Waldo Emerson—a philosophical visionary more complete than any other this nation has produced—identified two components to attaining personal power. One is to "drill." By this he meant training, rehearsal, education—the repeated application of a skill, over and over, the way a martial artist never stops working his routines. The other is "concentration." By this he meant you must target the energies of your training at a narrowly fixed aim. A pilot rehearses landings over and over so that he can guide his plane to safety in any conditions. A marksman aims at a bull's-eye. A dancer trains his or her body to respond to choreography and rhythm and to have second-nature command over fundamental movements.

But the cycle of *drilling* and *concentration*, Emerson wrote, is predicated by a more basic trait: physical health. Without physical health, nothing is possible. By "health" he did not mean the absence of disability; but rather the capacity to perform and act without chronic illness diverting your mind and will. If you lack wellness, your pursuit of corrective health will likely require almost all of your energies. This is a tough and unavoidable condition of life. This is why, from the healing ministry of Christ through the advent of the mental-healing movement in mid-nineteenth-century New England, virtually every expression of a spiritually based path to self-realization and refinement has been predicated on recovery and health.

So let us ask plainly: Can positive-mind metaphysics cure illness? This is an urgent matter to many people. I wish I could offer a simple affirmative answer or reassurance. I cannot. No honest dealer can. But I can offer insight that brings some perspective to the matter and, I hope, maximizes your chances of wellness.

One of the most alluring and provocative passages in Scripture is from Psalm 82:6–7: "Ye are gods but ye shall die as princes." For generations, New Thoughters have embraced the first part and remained mute about the second. But you cannot have the fruit without the pit; the pit is the seed for new fruit, or expanded realization. It does not mean abrogating the metaphysical search to acknowledge that we operate within physical limitations. This fact is made overly complex by some New Thought writers, who make needlessly ponderous (and unverifiable) claims that we exit at the perfectly appointed moment (have they ever visited a cancer ward?), or that all health is subjected to one Mental Super Law, which is ours to wield like a potter's wheel. This is unsupportable. We exist under many laws and forces, including physical decline and eventual demise. "Ye shall die as princes"—we are potential princes, but we dwell in fragile and temporary palaces.

So, can positive-mind therapeutics help cure illness? Is there hope? Yes. Firstly, we live in an era of almost miraculous new findings in the field of placebo studies. Researchers from previous generations, even those who experienced the bounding growth of placebo science following World War II, could not have fathomed the surge of insights being experienced in the twenty-first century.

- In July 2002, researchers in the *New England Journal of Medicine* reported the effectiveness of placebo surgery: participants from the Houston Veterans Affairs Medical Center received mock arthritic knee operations—involving just a benign incision— and experienced substantially similar rates of relief, and vastly reduced recovery time, as patients who received standard invasive arthritic knee surgery. (Researchers have speculated that the placebo response might be the only cause for reported relief in such operations.)

- In 2010, Harvard Medical School researchers conducted an unprecedented "honest placebo" study in which an openly sham pill brought lasting relief to sufferers of Irritable Bowel Syndrome. Subjects knew they were receiving an inert substance, yet 59 percent reported relief (compared to 35 percent in the control group). What was happening? It may be that a patient's belief in the very possibility of mental therapeutics is sufficient to enact the self-healing response.

- Another Harvard Medical School study in 2014 reported that migraine sufferers experienced improved results from their prescriptions when they were supplied with positive information about a drug. This suggests that the placebo effect is always operative, working not only in conjunction with inert substances, but also affecting a patient's experience of traditional drugs and therapies.

- In a 2007 study, Harvard psychologist Ellen Langer reported that hotel maids experienced weight loss and reduced blood pressure when taught to understand that their daily work routine had significant aerobic benefits. Once these facts were established, within four weeks subjects lost weight *without* changes to their work habits or personal lives, and compared to no changes in a control group.

- In other studies by Langer (these the subject of later controversy but their results never fundamentally refuted*) elderly subjects experienced physical and mental improvements—including

---

*See "What If Age Is Nothing but a Mind-Set?" by Bruce Grierson in the *New York Times Magazine,* October 22, 2014. Researchers often dispute older studies, such as Langer's 1981 aging study, based on newer standards of methodology. But this phenomenon affects our view of all past clinical work, as it will affect how future researchers view today's practices, since methods inevitably progress.

increased strength and flexibility, recovered memory and cognitive function, and improved mood and vitality—when immersed in nostalgic settings filled with stimuli from their youth, including vintage books, music, and movies. Settings that evoked feelings of youth actually seemed to summon the reappearance of youthful traits, extending even to improved eyesight.

- Clinicians writing in August 2016 in the research journal *Nature Medicine* reported that by stimulating the "reward system" in the brains of mice—in which a payoff is anticipated—they strengthened the animals' immune responses. These findings suggest that even a generalized state of positive expectancy may have immunological benefits, and also identify a key link—*reward anticipation*—in the action of the placebo response.

The only commentators who truly have no idea what is happening in this field are those who are certain that they know what is happening. The one certainty we can derive from the new findings in placebo science is that the energies of the mind play a greater and more varied role in health than clinicians previously realized. The data stream allows us to document this phenomenon but not fully explain it. The common denominator in all placebo experiments is the presence of hopeful expectancy. Whether this arrives through moral support, credible encouragement, education, religious belief, anticipation of reward, or a combination, the arousal of expectancy is the catalyzing event. Belief is the fee of actualization.

Critics call belief a delusion. But they misunderstand what is occurring. A delusion is a limiting, diverting mind-set. If your belief does not deter you from using recognized medical means—in other words, if it does not proscribe your therapeutic possibilities—it cannot be called delusion. It is, rather, a complement. My recommendation is to use the best in allopathic medicine, pharmaceuticals, validated alternative therapies, and palliative care—along with prayer, meditation, visualization, and affirmation (methods we explore in the following chapter). Take a D-day approach: throw everything at the problem.

Traditional religion has long affirmed this outlook. In her 2009 study *Medical Miracles*, hematologist Jacalyn Duffin noted: "To my surprise as a doctor and a historian, I quickly learned that the Vatican does not and never did recognize healing miracles in people who eschew orthodox medicine to rely solely on faith."

The early days of positive-mind metaphysics were dominated by health concerns. The quality of medical care in the nineteenth century was often abysmal, even by premodern standards, something I consider in my *One Simple Idea*. But many patients today continue to seek faith-based complements to medical treatment. What can positive-mind metaphysics offer? I replied to the following letter in July 2015:

Hi Mitch,

I was just wondering if you had anything to help someone with a spinal cord injury. Have you ever used your methods to heal or improve a spinal cord injury?

Thank you for the information.

Dear _____,

I'm a firm believer in taking an "all and everything" approach—combining prayer, affirmations, meditation, and the best in mainstream and (if appropriate) alternative medical care. For meditation my personal choice is Transcendental Meditation, which I highly recommend. You can locate a teacher online. For affirmations, I admire the work of French mind theorist Émile Coué; if you like I can send you an info sheet on his method—which is very simple. [This and other methods mentioned here appear in the next chapter.] Regarding prayer, I endorse a very ecumenical approach and work with varied traditions. I recommend the Divine Mercy devotion (you can find this online) and the Miraculous 54-Day Rosary

Novena (I can send you info or you can find it online). And, of course, always use the best available medical care.

I think we live under many laws and forces—spiritual, physical, emotional, mental—and I would enlist all of these forces in pursuit of recovery. I wish you every good thing.

I will be saying a prayer for you tomorrow at 3 p.m. EST.

Very best,
Mitch

I share the perspective of Norman Cousins who wrote in *Anatomy of an Illness* in 1979: "Not every illness can be overcome. But many people allow illness to disfigure their lives more than it should. They cave in needlessly. They ignore and weaken whatever powers they have for standing erect."

Now, I do *not* discount the possibility of extraordinary—even miraculous—episodes of recovery pertaining to the mind. And when I write "mind" I use an open-ended definition. If the mind has extra-physical dimensions, if it goes beyond cognition and motor commands, which I argue that it does, then the mind opens onto vistas that the human search, while millennia old, has only begun to detect.

Since the mid-1960s, a handful of physicians and clinicians have been making an effort to document one of the most astounding yet verifiable facts in the field of cancer research: spontaneous remissions of terminal cases.[*] In researching this question at the New York Academy of Medicine library, I found that about twenty such cases appear in world medical literature each year.[†] Many cases, clinicians agree, are probably unreported. Based on estimated spontaneous regression rates

---

[*]See *Spontaneous Regression of Cancer* by T. C. Everson and W. H. Cole (W. B. Saunders, 1966).
[†]"The Spontaneous Regression of Cancer: A Review of Cases from 1900 to 1987" by G. B. Challis and H. J. Stam, *Acta Oncologica* 29, Fasc. 5 (1990).

worldwide—about one out of every one hundred thousand cases of cancer*—it can be extrapolated from the number of new cancer cases reported annually in the United States that about fifteen episodes of spontaneous regression occur here each year. There is no consensus around the causes of spontaneous remissions. Clinicians hypothesize that in rare cases patients may have been misdiagnosed, or patients may have been suffering from a severely impaired immune system, which, for reasons unknown, was restored to normal or exceptional functioning, perhaps due to the healing of an undetected virus or infection. Clinicians also acknowledge the possibility of mental therapeutics.

"Of all possible mechanisms cited for regression," wrote G. B. Challis and H. J. Stam in the journal *Acta Oncologica* in 1990, "the psychological is the only category which is not clearly biological." In surveying the extant literature, these researchers found that "only three authors are primarily responsible for reports of regressions by psychological means in the scientific literature"—and only one, Australian psychiatrist and researcher Ainslie Meares, "provided sufficient information to be able to include the cases in our tables."

Ainslie Meares (1910–1986) presented a special case in point. In the 1970s and '80s, Meares oversaw and published research on the practice of intensive meditation by terminally diagnosed cancer patients for whom traditional treatments, such as chemotherapy, had been discontinued; in other cases he employed intensive meditation (sometimes three hours a day) with patients who had "advanced cancer" but were still undergoing treatment. He documented notable therapeutic episodes in both groups.

In a 1980 report on seventy-three patients who had advanced cancer,† Meares found that intensive meditation helped relive pain, depression, and anxiety, and contributed to a more peaceful and dignified death when cases proved terminal. In addition, Meares wrote of cancer

---

*"Spontaneous Regression of Cancer: A Review of Cases," Challis and Stam.
†"What Can the Cancer Patient Expect from Intensive Meditation?," *Australian Family Physician* (May 1980).

patients who undergo intensive meditation: "There is reason to expect a ten percent chance of quite remarkable slowing of the rate of growth of the tumour, and a ten percent chance of less marked but still significant slowing. The results indicate that patients with advanced cancer have a ten percent chance of regression of the growth."

Meares also documented a small, but not isolated, number of cases where terminally diagnosed patients spontaneously regressed while following a protocol of intensive meditation. In an article in *Australian Family Physician* in March 1981,* he described the case of a fifty-four-year-old married woman with two grown children who had recovered from breast cancer following meditation. When a mastectomy failed to check her cancer growth, the patient had refused chemotherapy and embarked on a program of anabolic steroid use and natural supplements (which Meares neither studied nor endorsed). She began to show healing after seeing Meares for meditation sessions each weekday for one month, using a technique of sitting still and experiencing her "essential being," as he described it, without concentration of any kind. (In general, Meares restricted his research to subjects who had seen him for at least twenty meditation sessions of one hour or more daily. Although he does not specify the length of time this fifty-four-year-old woman sat daily, some of his patients meditated up to three hours a day.) He wrote of her remission:

> A single case, considered by itself, may not be very convincing. But if we consider the particular case in conjunction with other patients who have responded in similar fashion, the relationship of treatment and outcome becomes more clearly established. In other words, the present case is not an isolated incident. It is one of a series of cases of regression of cancer following intensive meditation in some of which the regression has been more complete than in others.

---

*"Regression of the Recurrence of Carcinoma of the Breast at Mastectomy Site Associated with Intensive Meditation."

I was informally describing all this one evening in 2016 to a research pathologist at Harvard Medical School who specializes in breast cancer. I broached the topic with him of these rare but documented cases of spontaneous remission. Some cases, as noted, are evidently autoimmune related; but we also talked about the correlations with intensive meditation. The researcher's response: "I have to be objective. But I have noticed that patients who display a positive attitude toward their treatment tend to do better. My colleagues have noticed this too. We don't know why that is."

It is difficult to write about this kind of subject, even inconclusively, because it tends to polarize. Readers with New Age sympathies are apt to seize upon such discussions as validation that mind-body medicine, perhaps coupled with some kind of detox program, represents the royal road to health. Meares said no such thing, and he was scrupulous, as any responsible researcher would be, not to plant false hopes. Yet there is an equal and opposite extreme, in which a physician or a skeptic (usually a journalist) approaches such a discussion without a sense of proportionality, assuming that *any* such talk is akin to propagating groundless "miracles" or wishful thinking. (Indeed, after I had noted the Harvard researcher's remarks on social media, another research physician I know objected that we were entertaining rash conclusions; he missed our expressed intent to avoid conclusions or leading questions but rather to frame a discussion.)

I want to give the final word to Meares, because his tone and carefulness exhibit what is needed today in the body-mind-spirit and New Thought culture. He wrote this in "Cancer, Psychosomatic Illness, and Hysteria" in the *Lancet* of November 7, 1981:

In medicine we no longer expect to find a single cause for a disease; rather we expect to find a multiplicity of factors, organic and psychological. It is not suggested that psychological reactions, either psychosomatic or hysterical, are a direct cause of cancer. But it seems likely that reactions resembling those of psychosomatic illness and conversion hysteria operate as causes of cancer, more so in some cases than in others, and that they operate in conjunction with the known chemical, viral, and radiational causes of the disease.

This is, to me, the kind of voice our society needs to cultivate generally—in politics, spirituality, and medicine. It is the voice that sustains a question, which is the vantage point from which all new understanding is gained.

CHAPTER FOUR

METHODS
IN MIND POWER

Up to this point, I have used several terms in connection with positive-mind mechanics: *affirming, visualizing, meditating,* and *praying.* Historically, these are seen as the core methods for harnessing the mind's formative energies. We will now explore the nature of each technique, and how to most powerfully use it.

AFFIRMING

If you suffer from depression or are grieving, the most dangerous time of day is the "wee hours" of the morning, when you hover between sleep and wakefulness. In this stage, sometimes called the hypnagogic state, you are cognizant of surroundings and stimuli—but sleep researchers have found that your faculties of logic and perspective are at an ebb, which can invite a sense of surrealism and allow your fears and worries to run riot.

Equally delicate are those nighttime moments just before nodding off, when you balance between wakefulness and sleep. Here, too, your conscious awareness is precarious and richly imaginative: Your mental pictures morph, bend, and unfold like the images of a Salvador Dali painting.

At times of both drifting to sleep and awakening, the state of hypnagogia presents us with what might be considered prime time for channeling the energies of thought. At such periods, we retain a modicum of choice-making abilities, but are deeply relaxed—even immobilized—and emotionally vulnerable, which can be used to our advantage. Emotional vulnerability, provided that it is purposefully directed and not carried off by phantom fears, is the ideal state for using affirmations and visualizations to impress the subconscious and spur subtle abilities of thought.

Mind theorists have long detected the potentials of this "in between" stage. The mystic teacher Neville described using the 3 p.m. hour—when he felt drowsy following lunch (assisted by wine; Neville was no ascetic)—to take a nap and use the bridge to sleep to form mental pictures. Serious psychical researchers, such as Charles Honorton (1946–1992), found that instances of ESP or telepathy are higher when subjects are placed into a state of comfortable hypnagogia, involving sensory isolation and relaxation, perhaps wearing white-noise headphones, sinking into a recliner, and fitted with eyeshades. (We will return to Honorton's research.) French hypnotherapist Émile Coué (1857–1926) prescribed using the hypnagogic state to recite his famous mantra: "Day by day in every way, I am getting better and better." His formula was to whisper it gently twenty times just before drifting off, and once more upon waking. Coué advised making a string with twenty knots to mark off your repetitions as if on rosary beads (you can also use your fingers). This is to avoid rousing yourself through the mental act of counting. Critics dismissed the simplicity of Coué's program; but he displayed prescient insights into the uses of hypnagogia.

Hypnagogia adds tremendous power to affirmations and visualizations—the two are intimately related—by making it easier to place emotional conviction behind them. Emotion is the building block of belief and the key to influencing the subconscious. Indeed, it is vital that your affirmation or visualization have emotional persuasiveness at the back of it—and that it is felt with conviction and integrity.

Too often in the New Thought world we conflate thoughts and emotions. But the two are very different and function on separate tracks. Reciting an affirmation without emotional conviction achieves nothing; in fact, it may do more harm than good by summoning disbelief and resistance. Unless you are trained in the art of method acting (which is actually a good tool for a New Thoughter), you may have no idea how to summon emotions. But the hypnagogic state is one of the rare times when almost anyone can use mental images to induce emotion. During hypnagogia, your mind's-eye images are very believable, for good or ill. It is a time when figment and reality, suggestion and certainty, easily blend.

I advise using the hypnagogic state to picture the achievement of a cherished aim. To do this, enact in your mind a small, pleasing drama that suggests attainment—i.e., that the thing you want has *already* come to pass—such as a congratulatory handshake from your employer or you holding an award. You might accompany it by an unspoken, imagined statement, such as an effusive *thank you*. Allow yourself to drift to sleep, or enter wakefulness, while enacting this mental drama. *Feel the pleasure of your attainment.* This serves to condition the mind, which, when properly charged with a goal, can function as a homing device, somewhat like a heat-seeking missile, and hence direct your faculties in the direction of your desire.

But more than just that is happening: The mind, in a supple and creative state, is, I believe, a co-creator of events; it participates in a kind of macro thought field of which we have gained glimpses in ESP or psychical experiments. In the 1980s, the ESP researcher Honorton engaged a series of heavily juried and validated trials called the *ganzfeld* (German for "whole field") experiments."* These experiments induced hypnagogia by placing a subject—the "receiver"—into conditions of pleasurable sensory deprivation, generally in a comfortable isolation booth. Another subject—the "sender"—would sit outside of the booth and attempt to

---

*For an overview of Honorton's ganzfeld experiments, see *An Introduction to Parapsychology,* 5th edition, by Harvey J. Irwin and Caroline A. Watt (Garfield, 2007).

mentally "transmit" images to the receiver. In many individual cases, and in a meta-analysis, the ganzfeld experiments demonstrated higher-than-average hit rates. Honorton theorized that sensory quietude heightened ESP latencies.

Psi-research critic Ray Hyman, a psychologist at the University of Oregon, collaborated with Honorton on a paper that validated the experiment's research methodology and lack of "pollution," i.e., mistakes or corruption in the data.* Hyman rejected the conclusion that non-physical data conveyance was present, but he acknowledged the need for further study. Whatever one's viewpoint, *something* of significance was occurring during the ganzfeld experiments. This something may hold the key to part of what occurs during the positive-thinking experience.

It is possible that our minds are like ever-operative transmitting stations. We are always "broadcasting" what we want, seeking avenues of possibility and collaborators. When you begin to use your mind according to the methods in this book, you might happen upon "meaningful coincidences," in the form of fortunate accidents, intuitive connections, and portentous discoveries. If we are always scanning for resources, it is possible that this "signal" is heightened when we steadily affirm and visualize our desires during the hypnagogic state. (I deal later with how to distinguish these from mere "chance" occurrences.)

It may be that artists, entrepreneurs, and creative people demonstrate a constructive form of obsessive thought by constantly dwelling on their aims, including during hypnagogia. I once delivered a talk on the life of medical clairvoyant Edgar Cayce at a wealthy retirement community in upstate New York. After the talk, an audience member approached me and asked: "How do you sleep at night?"

"Excuse me?" I replied, thinking that I was being accused of something.

"How do you sleep?" she repeated—explaining that my mind always seemed to be running.

---

*"A Joint Communiqué: The Psi Ganzfeld Controversy" by Ray Hyman and Charles Honorton, *Journal of Parapsychology* 50 (December 1986).

Once I understood her, I realized that, by constantly thinking of projects, aims, and possibilities, I might be regularly using hypnagogic transmission, attracting people who can lend a hand or meet me halfway. As it happens, I *do* sleep at night—though only with the assistance of exercise and meditation. This woman instinctively grasped that my "idea factory" is constantly whirring, including during highly sensitive periods.

Not all affirmations, or statements of intent, need to occur in the hypnagogic state. You can commit a statement to paper and recite it during waking hours. Writing down an affirmation, goal, or intent has special potency. The physical act of writing—not on a device but with a pen or pencil to produce a tangible document—not only helps fix something in your awareness but is, in effect, the first step to actualizing the thought. Committing an idea to paper, in however nascent a form, brings something concrete into your world. It vivifies your ideas, renders them tactile, and helps establish your proprietorship over them. (After spending considerable time working out an idea on paper, you may want to "nest" it on a device.)

A persistent and misdirected debate runs through New Thought: Should affirmations be rendered in the present tense ("I am") or future tense ("I will")? Some argue that the future tense pushes off your aims to an unrealized point in time and perpetuates belief in current circumstances. Is there a right way to affirm?

There is not. You should use whatever language feels most authentic and natural and helps sustain your emotive passion. If you have difficulty believing that you possess something right now, and it feels more natural to locate it in the future, then do so. There is no wrong way of enunciating a goal.

The life of groundbreaking science fiction novelist Octavia Butler (1947–2006) is a case in point. Butler grew up in a working-class, African-American household in Pasadena, California, in the 1950s and '60s. Awkward, shy, and unusually tall for her age, she felt isolated from other kids. In her solitude, Butler developed voracious reading habits and a burning desire to write. She went on to become sci-fi's first widely recognized African-American woman writer, gaining popularity and critical acclaim.

Archivists at the Huntington Library in Los Angeles discovered among the novelist's papers a remarkable and prescient rendering of her personal vision, which she handwrote in 1988 in New Thought tones: "I shall be a bestselling writer. . . . This is my life. I write bestselling novels. . . . I will find the way to do this. So be it! See to it!" Butler used both future and present tenses in her vision—she wrote her intentions without getting distracted by form. Examine Butler's full affirmation:

I shall be a bestselling writer.

After *Imago*, each of my books will be on the bestseller lists of LAT, NYT, PW, WP, etc.

My novels will go onto the above lists <u>whether publishers push them hard or not</u>, whether I'm paid a high advance or not.

This is my life. I write bestselling novels. My novels go onto the bestseller lists on or shortly after publication. My novels <u>each</u> travel <u>up</u> to the <u>top</u> and they <u>stay on top</u> for months (at least two). Each of my novels does this.

<u>So be it!</u>

<u>See to it!</u>

I will find the way to do this. So be it! See to it!

My books will be read by millions of people!

I will buy a beautiful home in an excellent neighborhood.

I will send poor black youngsters to Clarion or other writer's workshops.

I will help poor black youngsters broaden their horizons.

I will help poor black youngsters go to college.

I will get the best of health care for my mother and myself.

I will hire a car whenever I want or need to.

I will travel whenever and wherever in the world that I choose.

My books will be <u>read</u> by <u>millions of people</u>!

So be it! See to it!

Read her lines again and again. Memorize them. Let their clarity permeate your mentality. Notice how a great artist combined ideals, vision, and sweat equity. And how she implicitly understood that there are no requisites or formalized ways of expressing the language of your desire.

When you hit upon and write down the right affirmation—a combination of mission, passion, and realistic ambition*—it serves to heighten and bring texture to your aim. You begin to weigh and judge your relationships, time, and commitments based on whether they constructively contribute to your aim. Like a vow of marriage, a contract of services, or even a declaration of war, the right affirmation enunciates your commitment and sharpens your intent. Hours spent crafting and recrafting the right statement of intention are never wasted. Never neglect to write it down.

VISUALIZING

Visualizations occupy a central place in New Thought and relate closely to affirmations. As noted above, the idea is to picture and feel what you wish to possess or achieve. If you want to look at matters from a

---

*I deal with the question of realism in chapter 5.

strictly psychological perspective, I believe that a mental picture, like an affirmation, focuses the mind on an aim and tends to make you more aware of people, ideas, correspondences, and possibilities that bring you closer to your goal. Such practices may also, over time, redirect neural pathways to facilitate certain physical or motor aptitudes, particularly if you are an athlete, dancer, musician, or designer.

You've probably noticed times when a focused thought or image—perhaps in the form of a deeply held conviction or burning question—seemed to bring you in proximity to people and situations related to what you were concentrating on. I'll venture that you can think of episodes when a person, object, or desired circumstance just "showed up." I suggest that this may not be simply because you were more aware of relevant circumstances, or that you were willfully seizing upon confirmations of a preexisting idea (a phenomenon researchers call "confirmation bias"). As with the events observed in the ganzfeld experiments, you may be conveying your images in a mind-to-mind fashion, reaching out to those who can offer assistance or information. The means of transmission might hinge upon greater or lesser degrees of ESP, a subject with serious implications for New Thought.

The term ESP, for "extrasensory perception," was popularized in the early 1930s by Duke University researcher J. B. Rhine (1895–1980), one of my intellectual heroes. Rhine conducted tens of thousands of trials in which subjects attempted to "guess" which card was overturned on a five-suit deck. Certain individuals persistently scored higher-than-average hits. These few percentage points of deviation, tracked across decades of testing, demonstrated some form of anomalous transfer of information—either that, or the manner in which we compile clinical statistics is flawed in some way that we do not understand.

Like researcher Charles Honorton, a onetime protégé of his, Rhine labored intensively, and under the scrutiny of critics, to safeguard against corruption in his data—so much so that his card experiments far exceeded the controls of most clinical trials, including those for today's commonly prescribed drugs. Mathematician Warren Weaver, a former president of the American Association for the Advancement of Science, who directed the allocation of hundreds of millions of dollars in medical research grants for the Rockefeller Foundation and Alfred P. Sloan Foundation, examined Rhine's methodology and remarked in 1960: "I find this whole field intellectually a very painful one. And I find it painful essentially for the following reasons: I cannot reject the evidence and I cannot accept the conclusions."* Weaver, like Hyman, did not share the psi research community's views on ESP; but, as a scientist, he refused to shut the door on the matter. Contemporary researchers including Dean Radin of the Institute of Noetic Sciences (IONS) in Northern California and Daryl J. Bem of Cornell University continue this work today, and Rhine's research center remains active.

Once more, think back to periods in life where you visualized, and held in mind, a particular need. Perhaps you urgently needed to reach a key person or required some piece of information. And then, something occurred: a deeply meaningful coincidence, one with such emotional import that it was laden with significance for you. Now, some statisticians argue that because the world is so vast and so brimming with possibilities, seemingly "unlikely" or coincidental events are actually not as fantastical or odds busting as they may appear.

Warren Weaver himself, in a private letter to Rhine of February 22, 1960,† noted that events with an "exceedingly small probability" do occur, and even ordinary events require a singular confluence of circumstances. "In other words," Weaver wrote, "the actual events of life are, individually considered, almost miraculously improbable."

Although this is true from a statistical perspective, I offer two considerations: (1) Rhine documented repeat events—not one improbability "individually considered," but a pattern that effectively exceeded

---

*For Weaver's assessment, see Stacy Horn's penetrating study of Rhine, *Unbelievable* (HarperCollins/Ecco, 2009).

†Weaver's letter and Rhine's reply (noted below Weaver) are from the Parapsychology Laboratory Records, 1893–1984, Rare Book, Manuscript, and Special Collections Library, Duke University, Durham, North Carolina.

all probability—and, more importantly to our purposes here, (2) statistics can measure the odds of an event but not the emotional gravity or individualized meaning attached to it. For example, if I meet a hero of mine on the street, it may be, statistically speaking, unremarkable. But if I meet that hero just before making a vital decision—and I am critically influenced or inspired by that person—the factors involved become more remarkable. In a reply to Weaver of March 15, 1960, Rhine noted: "the amount of confirmation required will depend upon various things, not the least among them being the question of how surprising or how unlikely a hypothesis appears to be."

In short, Rhine and his ESP experiments suggest that considerably propitious events may be far more than "happy accidents." They may be the ESP of daily life. Carl Jung called them "synchronicities." I will return to the correlations that Rhine hypothesized between mental picture, mood, and extraphysical mentality.

Mental visualizations require consistency and feeling. They are not always easy to sustain. (In the first season of *The Sopranos,* the character Christopher tells his girlfriend, "You know how I use the technique of positive visualization?" She responds, "I know you *talk* about it.") In 2016, a woman wrote me about difficulties she was experiencing in maintaining a mind-picture of a desired reality, and of feeling her way into it, as Neville Goddard prescribed. "The one problem I've been having in using Neville's method," she wrote, "is the *feeling* part. I can picture a scene in my mind, and a lot of times vividly, but the corresponding emotion isn't there. And that's when the fear of not ever having changes appear in my life grips me. Any suggestion?"

Neville's method is to picture a small, satisfying scene that implies achievement of your aim. You are to bask in the emotions of your goal having been reached as you rerun this small scene in your mind. I replied to the correspondent: "I recommend using Neville's visualization methods when your emotions are already on your side, i.e., when you're already in a vital, joyous, or at least contented mood. Don't struggle with it when you feel anxious. Even if it means walking away for a few hours, or a few days, you can always come back. Let your mood match the wished-for thing."

Pitting our minds against our moods is, as a great teacher once observed, like pitting steam power against nuclear power. The emotions win every time. Better to *use* emotions rather than try to counter them. Allow yourself to stop and wait, however long it takes, for when you can ride your emotional wave, so to speak, rather than attempt to reverse it.

My correspondent wrote back to me, "Sometimes I just want to see the results so much. And having real needs often brings on that 'desperate' feeling, which always seems like it negates my attempts at relaxing into the state."

I experience that very frustration myself, I told her. The *wanting* is so strong. It breeds impatience. But we needn't be afraid to let go of a cherished goal for a short time, or allow ourselves to casually relax without aim or focus, sometimes through watching a movie or taking a night out, or some other diversion. I actually think that when we *truly* want something we never forget it—it's always there hovering in the background. It's fine to not focus too closely on visualization until the moment arrives when our mood is in the proper state. The desire will be there. We never lose any ground.

Sometimes a state of ease and hopeful expectancy is itself sufficient to bring us what we want, or to help. In October 2016, I was on a month-long sabbatical from my publishing job and was completing some writing projects. I reached a moment where I had concluded three important projects, and I felt a sense of interval. I wasn't sure what to begin next. I needed a push in the right direction. It occurred to me, I'm not sure precisely from where, that a large mainstream news organization would reach out to me and ask me to write a piece. That is exactly what occurred. That same day, I received a call from an editor who told me that his colleague had been trying in vain to reach me (there was a minor email glitch). He put me in touch with the editor, who had for me what I considered, frankly, a dream assignment.

My expectant mood and the visual verity of the event were already in place. It happened quickly—within hours. Coincidence? Precognition? Mental attraction? I have no idea. My colleague Dean Radin, who has done remarkable experiments in precognition (which we'll examine), would probably suggest that this was an example of that phenomenon, made more likely by my being keyed up by a strong emotional association with the assignment. J. B. Rhine noted the importance of a subject feeling an emotional pitch during an experiment. One could consider, as I do later, that such episodes also suggest a nonlinearity of events, and that what transpires across a horizon of time does not run on an orderly track, but rather we "select" experiences from among innumerable possibilities.

In any case, I'm not sure that I can repeat that experience, or anything like it. Mental sensitivities can no more be "summoned" than feelings of love. This is why sensationalistic "tests," like magician James Randi's now-defunct million-dollar challenge to psychics in Vegas, rarely work. Because a phenomenon *occurs* doesn't mean it can come into being at any time.

I can say this much: Whatever the cause behind what happened, even if "coincidental," it didn't feel ordinary. It was charged with emotion, portent, and, by my reckoning, considerable unlikelihood, especially in the proximity of events. But I really do not know—and the point is not to reach conclusions. I'm not offering "scientific" steps or doctrine but meaningful experiences and articles of experimentation. The whole point is to experiment in the face of sometime impediments or inconsistencies. When dealing with ethical and spiritual philosophies, our only empiricism is of the inner variety. Evidence appears in outer events that comport with our mindscape.

A critic could rightly challenge: "Well, what about all the times when it *doesn't* work? And aren't we apt to forget, or 'edit out,' failures, in favor of events that seem portentous?" This is an extremely important cautionary note when entering into questions of mental causation. Be unsparingly strict with yourself. You are not merely looking for times when something "works," but rather for episodes that are demonstrably exceptional. This point was driven home to me in a story from my friend Dean Radin, a psychical researcher at the Institute of Noetic Sciences (IONS). Dean realized the *power of clarity* in attaining a personal goal. This is how he described it to me:

In 2009, we upgraded the EEG equipment in our lab to a 32-channel system in preparation for an experiment exploring whether experienced meditators' oft-reported experience of "timelessness" might be ontologically accurate rather than just a subjective time distortion. We asked the participants to meditate while they were exposed to a randomly timed light flash or audio tone stimuli. The idea was that if their awareness was genuinely spread out in time, including into the future, then perhaps just *before* the stimuli objectively occurred we'd see a pre-response in their brain activity. This experiment was following up on previous precognition studies investigating what we dubbed "presentiment" effects, i.e., unconscious physiological reactions to future events.

We recruited participants, ran the experiment, and collected a ton of data. Then the EEG analysis phase began. I surveyed software suitable for analyzing multichannel EEG data and found one that looked particularly good, called EEGLAB. This is a free, open source software suite used in thousands of academic neuroscience labs around the world. It uses Matlab, a high-end, general purpose programing language popular in scientific and engineering circles. I was not familiar with either EEGLAB or Matlab, but I knew that to do the analysis justice, I had to use these tools. However, I was responsible for several other projects and I didn't have a big block of time I could set aside just to learn how to use EEGLAB. I needed help.

My initial idea was to find a college student who was familiar with Matlab and willing to learn how to use EEGLAB. I asked my research assistant, Leena, to see if she could find someone like that. She asked me to be clearer on exactly what, or whom, I was looking for.

What I really wanted was an experienced neuroscientist who was familiar with EEGLAB, willing to analyze the data from our experiment for free, and also willing to take the risk to collaborate on a study of presentiment, which falls far outside the usual range of topics that most neuroscientists are willing to entertain. I wasn't sure that such a person even existed, or if they did how to go about finding them.

Leena said not to worry about it.

Two days later I received an email from a fellow who had attended a talk I gave a few years before. He wanted to come by and visit our lab. I said sure.

Turns out, this fellow was not only a bona fide academic neuroscientist (from UC San Diego), and not only an expert with Matlab, and not only wanted to volunteer his assistance—he was also the person *who developed and maintained EEGLAB!*

Arnaud Delorme has been part of the IONS staff ever since. He also maintains his appointment at UCSD, and he's a full professor at Toulouse University in France.

This is just one example of a dozen or so striking synchronicities I've experienced, all of which were related to my gaining crystal clarity on exactly what it was that I wanted or needed. After gaining clarity, it generally takes a few days to a few weeks for the vision to manifest.

PRAYING

The writer and religion scholar Michael Muhammad Knight saw Spike Lee's movie *Malcolm X* at age fifteen and began his conversion to Islam. "Can a movie," Mike wondered, "be sacred scripture?" I strongly believe that it can.

For me, one recent screen experience that verged on the spiritual was Jude Law's performance in the HBO miniseries *The Young Pope.* Law played a rebellious, archconservative, and fiercely individualistic young pontiff whose behavior no one could predict or control. His approach to prayer was to make demands on God and the saints: "You *must,* you *must,* you *must!*"

This form of prayer is not wholly out of step with Judeo-Christian tradition. The Bible is filled with episodes of the patriarchs and prophets bargaining, cajoling, and arguing with God: Cain protests (successfully) that his sentence is too harsh; Jonah voices displeasure with God for being given prophecies to propagate, only for God to reverse them; Job demands explanations for his miserable fate; Adam, after biting the apple, answers back to God in confusion and challenge.

In this light, the prayer style of the young pope, an orphaned Queens, New York, native named Lenny Belardo, comports with classical tradition. And Lenny's petitions appear to work. When everything around him is coming apart, when the faithful are demoralized by his harsh social dictates, and when Vatican apparatchiks are befuddled over his inscrutable priorities, Lenny delivers apparent miracles: bringing motherhood to an infertile young woman; mortally punishing a corrupt and abusive mother superior; and, earlier in life, healing a terminally ill neighbor.

Drama aside, I am a believer in petitionary prayer—that is, in asking, even demanding, something very specific from God or a saint, especially when you've made a significant personal sacrifice or struggled to uphold a classically sanctioned ethical teaching and also labored to validate the goodness and generativity of what you're requesting (it must be acknowledged, however, that such perspective is never fully ours).

The act of belief itself may be key to the outcome you experience. "I confess," William James wrote in his essay "Is Life Worth Living?" in 1895, "that I do not see why the very existence of an invisible world may not in part depend on the personal response which any one of us may make to the religious appeal. God himself, in short, may draw vital strength and increase of very being from our fidelity."

Now, some in the New Thought tradition—and Neville is the prime example—teach that *consciousness is God,* and that there is no one and nothing to whom to appeal beyond your own mind. "There is no God," Neville told listeners, "other than he who is your own wonderful human imagination." He chided people for praying to "these little pictures . . . little icons, little medals," as he put it, and insisted that if the word *God* summons for you a persona or entity outside of yourself, you have missed the true nature of things. But I seriously question the need for this division. If God is, in fact, awareness or consciousness, then why couldn't the mind-as-God model comport with humanity's collective awareness of a Higher Being to which an appeal can be made? I see no necessary conflict between a Divine Entity and the holiness of the mind: the latter is the branch and the former the tree, or the root. (And, I'm proud to add that as a New Thoughter, I wear the Miraculous Medal around my neck and use iconographic prayer cards.)

Moreover, I think that our network of psychologically conditioned fears and reactive emotions are sometimes impossible to break through without resorting to prayer. As a prerequisite to visualization and other methods, there are times when we *must* pray for respite from emotional habits, anxieties, and compulsions that becloud our psyches and sap our energies and enterprise. We need *help* to pierce the shell of our own psychological limitations in order to embark on the path of using the mind in a creative, generative manner.

I think it's vital to resort to prayer—in a direct appeal to the Higher—when we feel incapable of mustering a feeling-state of fulfillment or the ability to use our minds constructively. At times of brokenness, I believe it's efficacious and appropriate to throw yourself on your knees and beg God for something. Yes, beg. We're not supposed to do that in New Thought and positive-mind traditions. New Thought teaches "affirmative prayer," which means holding a thought or visual image, asking a Higher Power in deepest confidence to fulfill your needs, and "believing it is done." But why be bound to that convention? If you believe in the intercession of a Higher Power, as I do, use the language of your heart. Whether demanding, lovingly requesting, arguing, or pleading, there is no wrong way to pray, just as there is no wrong way to affirm.

Traditionally speaking, the Father is said to provide everything freely. But what if prayer is transactional? What do we *offer* God in exchange for the help we request? Historically, I believe it is entirely valid to attempt to make a "deal" with God. In a sense, the entire spiritual basis of Judaism involves man's fulfillments of God's injunctions in exchange for life, plenty, and security. This is the spiritual basis of the ancient practice of tithing. Some interpreters teach that we should tithe, pray, and give without expectation. Is that really possible—even as an ideal? You cannot fool yourself or God that you don't also harbor a yearning within. Even if the Creator adorns the lilies and feeds the birds, he has also mandated that you and I must earn and sow. Except for very subtle moments, it can be an act of artifice to pray free of all attachment, even if that attachment is simply to be shown your right path.

How do we bargain with God, as did the patriarchs? One time years ago I felt particularly desperate, and longed to escape a personal entanglement. I looked out across a small lake and prayed to God to deliver from me tormenting circumstances. *Do this for me,* I vowed, *and I will ever after strive to make my body and mind into an instrument for your will.* I was soon freed from these circumstances. I did a lesser job of keeping my end of the arrangement. But I was sincere, and I do think back to my vow whenever I am tempted to do something morally questionable.

In the last chapter, I mentioned the Miraculous 54-Day Rosary Novena. Now, every person from whatever background must find the language of prayer that suits his or her needs. I take a radically ecumenical approach, and personally recommend this highly rigorous prayer from the Catholic tradition, which has been a crucial help to me, as have other Catholic devotions. In short, it involves saying a traditional Rosary prayer in two cycles: first, in petition of your request for 27 days, and second, in thanksgiving for another 27 days, for a total 54 days.

In the traditional telling, on March 3, 1884, the gravely ill daughter of an Italian military officer experienced a visitation of the Virgin Mary. The ill girl was told: "Whoever desires to obtain favors from Me should make three novenas* in petition of the prayers of the Rosary, and three novenas of thanksgiving." She recovered. The faithful are told to say the cycle of thanksgiving prayers whether or not the request has been granted.

I have found this 54-day devotion extremely powerful—and practical. But do not even think of beginning it unless you are wholly committed. Saying a Rosary takes at least twenty minutes; hence, you are dedicating yourself to a minimum twenty-minute devotion for 54 consecutive days. If you feel a need acutely enough, you will be able to do it. If you find yourself skipping days or falling off schedule, you are probably not sufficiently focused on, or needful of, your objective.

My practice is to draw two grids of boxes, each nine rows long and three rows deep; the first is labeled, "I: In Petition" and the second, "II: In Thanksgiving." This gives you two cycles—petition and thanks— and fifty-four boxes to check off. You can avail yourself of any number of books and websites to walk you through the basics of the Rosary prayer itself.

I encourage a revolutionary approach to the possibilities of prayer. One of my heroes from modern Jewish tradition is a St. Louis, Missouri, rabbi named Louis Witt (1878–1950). In 1927, Witt addressed a gathering of the Central Conference of American Rabbis, which was then the largest rabbinical assembly in the nation. He wanted organized Judaism, and particularly its more liberal branches to which he was connected, to take seriously the benefits of prayer healing and mind metaphysics and to incorporate such things into the Jewish ministry. He delivered and defended a committee report to that effect. Witt's findings were almost hooted down by skeptical, sometimes caustic attendees. But on

---

*A novena is a prayer recited for nine consecutive days. Three novenas (3 x 9) are a 27-day cycle.

the final night of the gathering, he responded with a stunning response from the convention floor, preserved in meeting transcripts, in which he defended the therapeutic uses of prayer and mind power. Witt's statement is, to me, one of the great "lost" pieces of Jewish oration:

> Now it has been said, to my utter amazement, that this report and this recommendation is a departure from Judaism. If it is a departure from Judaism then I wish I could be in something else than in the Jewish ministry. I claim this is the very essence of all that is fine and beautiful in Orthodox Judaism. It is that which haunts those of us who have been raised in Orthodoxy. Orthodox fathers and mothers did not have our rationalistic attitude. To them God was a reality. I tested out this recommendation in New York City last week. I asked a group of Orthodox Jews to give me some of their experiences . . . I knew some of them very intimately. One of them told me that his daughter was very ill. He went to the Synagogue, he said, and had a prayer offered for his daughter. When he came home his daughter said to him, "Papa, I had a dream; I dreamed that my bed was carried to the altar and I began to feel better."
>
> The physician came the following day and although he had held out no hope the day before, he said, "Your child is going to get well."
>
> I have gone into the hospitals; I have heard Orthodox Jews say, "God will help." This is what saved Judaism, it has been that personal attitude to a God who was very, very near, who could heal the sick, who was always present in time of trouble, who was always doing a spiritual healing. . . .
>
> I am moved almost to smile—and if it were not so tragic I would smile—when I hear some of the rabbis say: Let us give the people more Judaism. You have been talking "more Judaism" ever since I have been a member of this Conference. What have you got? You have got nothing out of it because you have gone the wrong way. You are putting out new textbooks and you are giving more eloquent sermons on plays and novels and such things and you are talking before Rotary Clubs

and on International Peace, and all those things. They are incidental to religion. . . .

A woman came to me three weeks ago, in the depths of melancholia. I did not know what to do for her. I talked as a doctor might talk—but I wanted to offer prayer for that woman and I wanted that woman to feel that I myself have been helped. I have gone through the period of melancholia. I have been a neurasthenic because of an utter disillusionment with regard to certain things in the Jewish ministry, and the things to which I dedicated my life, and many of you have confessed to me in past years, and some of you confessed to me last night and the night before, that you are suffering the same thing. We are hiding these things from the world ... but the fact is that there is many a rabbi who is suffering from a sick soul and his soul is sick because life has meant frustration and disillusionment for him and we ourselves are not helped enough by the God that we preach—God is not near enough to us. . . .

I want this Conference to say that there is more power in religion than we are utilizing, and I want us then to proceed to utilize that power.

MEDITATING

There are many books on meditation, and I will not attempt here to consider the myriad methods, ancient and modern. I do believe that a meditative practice is vital to any spiritual journey. Among other things, meditation provides a kind of foundational starting point to ensure the best mental and emotional state for prayer and the use of mind therapeutics. In some cases, as seen in the research of psychiatrist Ainslie Meares, meditation itself is a decisive factor in healing.

My personal practice is Transcendental Meditation, an extremely relaxing, mantra-based form of meditation used for about twenty minutes in the morning and evening. Certified teachers can be found online. I highly recommend it, especially for people who have difficulty meditating. Other forms of meditation involve concentration, visualization, or "just sitting." Jon Kabat-Zinn, an impeccable researcher and thinker, has advocated a modified form of Buddhist-derived "just sitting" meditation, which he has popularized in his nationwide program of Mindfulness-Based Stress Reduction, or MBSR. This therapy has made impressive inroads in hospitals and mainstream medicine.

We like to think of meditation as "easy," but people sometimes underestimate the commitment required by meditation programs. As noted, some of Meares's patients meditated up to three hours daily. Even old-school self-help books, such as the 1960 *Psycho-Cybernetics* by Maxwell Maltz, M.D., prescribe meditative practices that require a commitment of at least one hour daily. Maltz, a pioneering cosmetic surgeon, taught that the individual could recondition his self-image through visualizations; he prescribed a half hour of "just sitting" meditation and another half hour of visualizing, in which the meditator pictured himself in peak performance. I am a great admirer of Maltz's program (as were a surprising range of figures, including first lady Nancy Reagan, actress Jane Fonda, and artist Salvador Dali), but it is important not to underestimate the commitment required. To begin such a program and then trail off for lack of time or discipline leads only to disappointment.

The point is: All of these practices can *work* provided you possess the one indispensable trait necessary for any successful program of self-development: impassioned commitment. The next chapter is dedicated wholly to that point.

CHANTING

I must explore one further method in using your mind as a causative instrument. It is, in effect, a mantra, originally written in Sanskrit and reformed into thirteenth-century Japanese: *nam myoho renge kyo*. Derived from the title of the classical Buddhist text the Lotus Sutra, the phrase means roughly: "I dedicate myself to the mystic law of cause and effect."

Chanting these four sounds—*nam myoho renge kyo*—is, in my experience, a practice of great power. It forms the heart of what is called Nichiren Buddhism, named for its founder, a thirteenth-century Buddhist priest, and practiced today by Soka Gakkai International, or SGI. I learned this chanting practice from someone who embodies its potential, Emily Grossman, an extraordinary mental-health professional.

Emily works at the Jewish Board, New York City's largest mental-health agency, where she trains employees and designs programs to aid the recovery of people with mental illness. She is distinctly effective at what she does because she understands what works from the perspective of her own recovery; and because she exemplifies the self-development principle of her spiritual practice.

Emily was diagnosed with bipolar disorder in 1996, just two months into her freshman year at Emory University. She was an ebullient young English major, a cheerleader, and an outgoing source of encouragement to others, yet her future seemed completely cut short. Emily's depression and panic attacks were so severe that she had to return home to New Jersey, where she experienced debilitating relapses that "broke through" her medication regimen. She suffered chronic thoughts of suicide and was so emotionally impaired that even the simple act of using an ATM machine was too difficult to manage. She found herself in and out of institutions and group housing and faced the very real prospect of a life of hospitalization.

Her younger sister, Pam, a thoughtful seeker and artist in her own right, handed Emily a copy of Anthony Robbins's self-help book *Awaken the Giant Within*. The book gave Emily a renewed sense of inner agency and pushed her to explore new possibilities in treatment. Many journalists and social critics regard Robbins, the mountainous life coach and purveyor of a *you-can-do-it* ethos, as something of a joke or huckster. He is no such thing. His message of self-possibility has saved lives. It opened Emily to options.

After bouncing in and out of jobs, Emily began to regain her footing and moved to New York City in 2005 to attend Teacher's College at Columbia University, from which she graduated the next year. At the time she half-jokingly told a classmate: "One day I'm gonna move to California and become a Buddhist." The friend replied: "Well, I'm from California and I'm a Buddhist and there's a meeting tonight." That marked her introduction to the practice of chanting *nam myoho renge kyo*.

"Very soon after I started practicing," Emily said, "I noticed that I was not as symptomatic—I wasn't feeling as depressed, in fact I was feeling happy. My medicine—which hadn't changed—was working better."

Like me, Emily grew up in a traditional Jewish household, in her case in Marlboro, New Jersey. I had a small orthodox bar mitzvah at a synagogue in New Hyde Park, Queens. Neither place is on the leading edge of New Age spirituality. But during her recovery, Emily experienced what I consider a breakthrough spiritual insight.

While she was experimenting with the ideas of Robbins, Deepak Chopra, Sharon Salzberg, and other alternative spiritual thinkers, and while at the start of her journey into Buddhism, she prayed to the God of her childhood "for a practice that reflected everything I was reading in those books." Rather than feeling that she was abandoning her childhood tradition, she *asked* her old tradition to open a new door for her: "I chanted and I said, 'God, I'm going to be talking to you in a different way now.'" Look at her remark again: "God, I'm going to be talking to you in a different way now." That statement displays great moral aptitude—and summarizes the challenge and courage of the New Age and positive-mind metaphysical practice. We are beings of radical ecumenism. Our myriad religious traditions, while using vastly different liturgies and sometimes harboring different aims, nonetheless serve as interlocking chains that can deliver us to what is intimately needed, even if a method or practice lies outside the borders of a tradition itself. The paradox of religion is that it can deliver you to solutions beyond its own premises.

That first evening in 2005 when Emily learned about chanting, a friend counseled: "Make a list of everything you want to change in your life." Emily recalled: "My desires were that I wanted a bad relationship to end; I needed a job right after school—and I needed to *keep* the job; I needed a car; and I wanted to live in Hoboken, New Jersey." These were immensely practical aims. Each was necessary (a car, a steady job—do you see why I refuse to judge "material" needs?) for assembling a life of independence while recovering from severe depression. Each came to her. And has remained with her.

As of this writing, Emily is thirty-eight and was diagnosed twenty years ago. She holds a graduate degree, lives a wholly independent existence (after more than ten hospitalizations and a stay in group housing), and maintains a distinguished career as an educator of mental-health professionals. "I've had no mania or depression in years," she told me in 2017. "I continue the meds—but I haven't changed them in more than a decade."

There is no question, in the eyes of Emily, her family, or myself, that chanting was an indelible factor in her recovery—one that not only stabilized her mood but also gave her new ideas about managing her symptoms and lifestyle. Why did her chanting work? Emily is pragmatic: "My impression is that chanting changed the neuro-pathways in my brain," providing new coping skills and ways of learning. But she concedes a more mystical possibility: "When I chant it puts me in rhythm with the greatest law of the universe"—that is, with a higher law of cause and effect.

Is there such a law? Whether you regard such a claim as metaphor or metaphysical fact, our sole means of measurement are the results found in the life of the practitioner. "We deal in actual proof," Emily said. "Not falling asleep in class or the job. Waking up on time. Relieved cognitive impairment"—these facts became part of her experience; they were the elements that allowed her to live independently.

Never limit your sense of possibilities or experimentation, especially when searching for a way out of a crisis or difficulty. A new idea or practice does not necessarily require giving up an old one. Emily did not discontinue her medications or treatment, and would encourage no one to do so. But in chanting *nam myoho renge kyo,* she found a practice that got her using her mind in a different way. That is the keynote of mind metaphysics: finding methods that make the mental act into a transformational and transcendent vehicle.

I argue that we can pierce a thin veil that separates mental and spiritual experience, thus using our minds not only as tools of cognition and motor function but as instruments of navigation into higher, unseen realms of psychology and cause and effect. We may be unable to see, describe, or fully identify these other spheres of existence—but their impact is palpably felt in our lives, as they were in Emily's.

CHAPTER FIVE

HOW TO MAKE A MIRACLE

This is the most important chapter in this book. If you take nothing else from what I've written, act on this chapter.

I have spent nearly twenty-five years of my adult life searching through the spiritual culture—during which time I have worked as a body-mind-spirit publisher, a historian of alternative spirituality, and an individual seeker, sampling and struggling with many of the ideas of self-liberation and self-development on the current spiritual scene (and working with the originators of some of these ideas).

This period of time has convinced me of the existence of one deeply powerful force, which can be cultivated as a means of advancing toward a sense of personal completeness, meaning, and self-purpose. We are always using this force, or more often are used by it, for good or ill. This force exerts a kind of gravitational pull, sometimes strong enough to flatten or abrogate mountains of circumstance, or erect new mountains, blocking our path to where we think we want to go. This force functions, either intimately or on a macro scale, as a catalyst for harmony or friction. It can deliver us to circumstances and events that surpass all conventional or natural expectation, which, as noted earlier, I define as a miracle.

What is this overlooked energy? *The power of one deeply felt wish.*

One finely honed, exclusively focused, and passionately felt desire. Something that feels to you like breath itself. Find this, and you will discover a power like none other available to you. This concept initially reached me through the example of one of the most impactful thinkers of the past century, Bill Wilson, cofounder of Alcoholics Anonymous.

In 1934, Bill was hospitalized and desperate for a solution to his compulsive and self-immolating drive to drink. His longtime friend Ebby Thacher introduced him to the principle that alcoholism requires a spiritual solution. Bill was able to stay sober by embracing the ideas that Ebby brought to him, including principles from the Christian fellowship the Oxford Group, psychologist Carl Jung, and philosopher William James. Bill used these ideas, and the experience of his own spiritual awakening, to lay the basis for the twelve steps and Alcoholics Anonymous.

Yet, tragically, Ebby Thacher, the man who ignited Bill Wilson's interest in spiritual self-help, soon relapsed into drunkenness. Ebby spent much of his remaining life in a battle with alcohol, often ill and destitute. When Ebby died in 1966, he was sober but living as a dependent at a recovery center in upstate New York. Bill regularly sent him checks to keep him going. Not that Bill's legs were always strong. He continually struggled with depression and chain-smoking. But he *did* attain his life's goal. Until he died in 1971, he never drank again.

Why did one man remain sober and another relapse?

Bill's wife, Lois, in a passage from her memoir, *Lois Remembers*, described, in an understated manner, the difference she saw between the two men. In so doing, Lois illuminated a mystery, maybe even *the* mystery, of human nature:

> After those first two years . . . why did Ebby get drunk? It was he who gave Bill the philosophy that kept him sober. Why didn't it keep Ebby sober? He was sincere, I'm sure. Perhaps it was a difference in the degree of wanting sobriety. Bill wanted it with his whole soul. Ebby may have wanted it simply to keep out of trouble.

Bill wanted it with his whole soul. That is the key. Within the parameters of physical possibilities, you receive what you "want with your whole soul"—whether inner truth, a personal accomplishment, relationships, or whatever it is. Excluding some great countervailing force, and for either ill or good, the one thing that you want above all else is *what you get.* This may beg dispute. People claim that they have *not* received what they want in life. But we can fool ourselves. Sometimes our memory gets clouded over or rearranged during an interval of time, and we emotionally disclaim or forget what we focused on intensively at an earlier stage of life.

Taking a leaf from Goethe's *Faust,* Ralph Waldo Emerson, in his 1860 essay "Fate," noted this dynamic—leading to the popularized adage: *Be careful what you wish for, you just might get it:*

> And the moral is that what we seek we shall find; what we flee from flees from us; as Goethe said, "what we wish for in youth, comes in heaps on us in old age," too often cursed with the granting of our prayer: and hence the high caution, that, since we are sure of having what we wish, we must beware to ask only for high things.

Other times we are simply oblivious to what we want, telling ourselves internally what we think we should want (e.g., a nice family, a good home), but we actually harbor a *different* wish, one that we sometimes deny or fail to recognize when it presses at the walls of our awareness.

Positive-mind philosophy places a demand on us, one that we may think we've risen to but have never really tried. And that is: *To come to an understanding of precisely what we want.* When we organize our thoughts in a certain way—with a fearless maturity and honesty—we may be surprised to discover our true desires. A person who considers himself "spiritual" may uncover a deep wish for worldly attainment; someone who has labored to support the work of others may find that he has deeply unsettled yearnings of his own for self-expression;

someone who is very public or extroverted may realize that he really wants to be alone.

Recall scientist Dean Radin's story from the previous chapter. His research assistant told him he must first arrive at a vivid picture of what he wanted, which in his case was an experienced neuroscientist willing to analyze nontraditional data for free. Dean refined his focus to the *ends*. When you begin to identify your natural desires, you begin to distinguish the *means* from *the thing itself*. And the *thing itself* is everything.

This process is not a mental exercise alone. In Dean's case, a tremendous degree of effort and background work predicated his abilities of causation and visualization. His actions in all their forms—work, study, effort, enterprise—enlisted other possibilities, including the intellectual, physical, and extraphysical. His act of focus was the closing catalyst. You must hone your focus while pushing on the handles of a plow. Thought without labor is like faith without works: dead.

MILITARY STRATEGY AS SELF-HELP

The dynamic I've been describing—focusing and acting on a desire with singular commitment—plays out not only in the lives of individuals but also in the events of nations and civilizations. We saw this process at work historically in America's involvement in Vietnam, though in an inverted form.

Early in my career as an editor in the mid-1990s, I had the privilege of working with Colonel Harry G. Summers (1932–1999), a decorated Vietnam officer whose book *On Strategy* is considered perhaps the greatest analysis of why the United States lost in Vietnam. It became a kind of strategy bible among a cohort of young officers in the post-Vietnam era.

When I met Col. Summers, I was working toward establishing myself as an editor of political books, which can make my current role as a historian and publisher of alternative spirituality seem discursive.

Like lines on a map, however, the curves and switchbacks of a person's life are like the natural contours of any path. Today, I see how various aspects of my career converged, even the seemingly diffuse fields of military strategy and self-help.

A blunt and erudite man, Col. Summers argued that the U.S. army was entirely capable of winning the war against North Vietnam. None of the opposing circumstances were insurmountable, he wrote, and, contrary to popular perception, American forces almost always prevailed on the battlefield, often delivering withering blows that sent the enemy in flight and resulted in territorial gains.

So what, from a military perspective, went wrong?

The despoiling factor, Col. Summers maintained, is that the nation's political leadership failed to build "moral consensus" for the war among the American public. President Lyndon Johnson never asked Congress for a formal declaration of war, which many policymakers at the time viewed as an outdated formality. Without a formal declaration, and the political process underscoring it—which required making a case for a war and framing the attendant stakes and sacrifices—the public as a whole was never truly persuaded. Hence, policymakers lacked the consent and authority to undertake an overwhelming war effort, relying instead on Defense Secretary Robert McNamara's chimerical (and failed) notion of a "limited war." The result was quagmire and pointless carnage abroad, and moral confusion and opposition at home.

Year after year, the nation's political leadership authorized the army to more or less muddle along in a half-in and half-out effort, which eroded political support and frustrated commanders. Without popular support and a formal war declaration, Col. Summers wrote, the war never should have been fought to begin with.

What works in military strategy is the same as what works in all other areas of life. You must be "all in." You must select an ultimate goal to which you dedicate yourself with unreserved commitment—or don't do it at all. When you decide on your goal, then "burn the fleet";

throw yourself into it with totality. Reverse or change plans only when factual evidence or overwhelming circumstance requires it.

THE ONE THING

We like to think that we can balance everything in life. And we are, of course, faced with multiple and sometimes shifting demands. You likely want happiness at home, health for yourself and your family, material comfort for people around you, and so on. These are all sound. But you must take this self-knowledge I've been describing, and, accepting that life's needs are multiple, use it to dedicate yourself to your core aim. One well-selected aim will facilitate the others.

Your aim must be specific, concrete, and plain. It must be achievable, even if greatly bold. Beware of aims that are self-contradicting, such as traveling to exotic places while also raising young children. Or becoming a great leader while also having lots of leisure time. An aim is single-minded.

An example of this came to me in 1996, when I met a figure who soon exploded across the political scene. One afternoon, I spoke for several hours with now-Senator Cory Booker (D-New Jersey), who was then an eager and highly ambitious Rhodes scholar and student at Yale Law School. Mutual friends told me: "You've got to meet this guy; he's going to be president someday." He was earnest but studied, and deeply persuasive. I could see exactly what people meant. Cory quickly rose to become the nationally prominent mayor of Newark, New Jersey, and then a senator and prospective running mate for candidate Hillary Clinton (she chose Senator Tim Kaine).

As of this writing, in 2017, Cory is on the short list for any executive ticket to emerge from the Democratic Party. You will be able to see for yourself whether he becomes president, a role that peers foresaw for him—and that I am certain he foresaw himself—while he was in his twenties. Some were turned off by Cory's ambition. I was not. He knew precisely what he wanted and possessed the skills, intellect, and drive to attain it. In areas where he was lacking, he was willing to gain the needed skills. (He made easy, perhaps too easy, friends in finance, so fundraising was head started.) In short, Cory possessed a hugely ambitious but also actionable goal.

Contrary to many purveyors of spiritual self-help, I reject the notion that we can become *anything* we dream of. Not all desires are realistic. You must possess the willingness and ability to begin, and to forge ahead on your own. Your age, training, and education matter—as do geography, finances, and time. These are not to be seen as barriers— but they are serious considerations. Surprises do occur: The Caribbean nation of Jamaica did, in fact, produce an Olympic bobsledding team in 1988 (as depicted in the comedy *Cool Runnings*). And some significant actors did not land the roles for which they became known until middle age. Classically trained actor Jonathan Frid was about to leave the stage and begin working as a drama coach when, at age forty-two, he landed the iconic role of vampire Barnabas Collins on TV's *Dark Shadows*. You may recall actor Allan Arbus as the psychiatrist Sidney Freedman on the acclaimed sitcom *M*A*S*H*—he got that role at age fifty-five after working for most of his life as a photographer. So, I am not suggesting that you retreat before barriers; but just be cognizant and realistic about where you are, what is required, and your willingness, through hard times and good, to see your project through.

Do you want to be a professional actor—and do you maturely understand the years of hard-won training and dedication involved? Do you possess the natural talent, physical appearance, grace, and dexterity required? (By physical appearance I do not mean traditional good looks but a certain "something" that makes you distinctive.) Do you have the stomach and resilience for the tears, joys, terrors, and dedication that acting and the audition grind entails? Have you been to professional auditions and seen the competition you are faced with? Are you already doing some or all of this? Have you the means to? Is everything else in your life secondary to this? *Then write it down as your goal.*

In seeking a realistic sense of self-capacity and purpose, I have been guided by a passage from the Talmudic book Ethics of the Fathers: "Find that place where there are no men; go there; and there strive to be a man." This can be read on many levels. Here is one: You must find that place—literally, figuratively, or both—where your real abilities are needed; then go there to do your work.

Scan your life for areas where you have been especially able to solve things for yourself and others. Where you added to the net output of a product, business, or organization. Where you made a resoundingly well-received point or contributed a concrete improvement to something. Where you lightened a load on others or displayed a trait toward which people gravitated. Those are immensely valuable pieces of information.

Just wishing to be a math whiz, an athlete, or an astronaut is insufficient. You must have a unity, an integration between your wishes and some vital and developing capacity within yourself—something expressive of a role you can fill in life. There must be a concentration of energies and a development of inner capacities, as well as the deeply felt wish.

That was the nature of my path to becoming a writer. I began my writing career as a reporter working an overnight crime beat for the *Times Leader*, a daily newspaper in Wilkes-Barre, Pennsylvania. I hated it. First, I had to put up with the idiotic jokes: "*Is there any crime in Wilkes-Barre?*" (Answer: Yes. As I write these words, Wilkes-Barre, a part of our nation's former industrial belt, is being ravaged by a heroin epidemic.) More privately, I agonized over my decision to join a paper whose owners had several years earlier busted its union. I am prolabor, but I went there anyway. It was a gutless decision for which I've never fully forgiven myself. And the work of a police reporter didn't suit me. I disliked many of the area cops (as they did me), and I got tired of the suspicious attitude that many of the locals harbored toward outsiders. Although I delivered many outstanding stories, I would count the hours each night until my shift ended.

One evening I was chasing a story about a cop accused of rape. I was finding my way around the wall of "blue silence," in which police don't discuss a crime committed by one of their own. That night a city editor made the abysmal judgment call of pulling me off that important story in order to cover a local Irish festival. I grumbled over the decision but trudged off to the festival. Another reporter broke my story. While I was complaining about it in the newsroom the next day, a fellow reporter, a French woman displaced to Wilkes-Barre (this was straight out of a David Lynch movie), confronted me and said that I hadn't really wanted the story.

"What?" I asked. "How could you say that?"

"Look," she said, "I know that you were pissed off when Linda sent you to cover the Irish festival. But you should've refused. You should've said no. You didn't really want the cop story badly enough. You let it get taken from you."

I was flattened by the truth of what she said. I was sick inside—because I knew she was right. Later that night I returned to my apartment. I went stealthily because, among the other joys of my time there, I was being stalked by a violent street vagrant with a feral pit bull; I had exposed his assaults on other homeless people. Once inside, I locked the door, dropped to the floor, and prayed to God with everything in me that if what my colleague told me was true (and I knew it was) to either help me recommit to journalism or give me the resolve to get out of it. I would not hang around my field as a mediocrity.

I got out. I took a job in book publishing in New York City, a place I yearned to live. That proved a so-so compromise. I did all right and earned a decent enough living; but I didn't feel like I stood for anything. I wanted to be in front of the camera, literally and figuratively, not just facilitating the work of others. The years piled up—five, ten, fifteen—since I left behind writing in Wilkes-Barre (a lament rarely heard in American letters). I was restless and dissatisfied.

Then, in summer of 2003, something unexpected occurred. Two friends, Amanda Pisani and Randall Friesen, were running the positive-thinking monthly *Science of Mind*—and had landed a very big "get." All-Star pitcher Barry Zito, then with the Oakland A's, committed to an interview. Barry used positive-mind methods in his training, including affirmations, prayers, and visualizations. Inside the rim of his cap he pasted the mantra: "Be still and know." In 2002, the southpaw had gone from the near-bottom of the major leagues to winning more games in a single season than any American League pitcher since 1988. "Dude," he told a reporter, "that's not a coincidence."

Barry's father, Joe, and mother, Roberta, were themselves deeply into mind metaphysics, and had infused their son with similar values. He had since become one of the most talked about figures in baseball. My friends at *Science of Mind* realized this interview was a big opportunity, and they brought it to me as someone they could trust. I vowed not to disappoint them.

News features are often written passively: a string of quotes pasted together with a little associative material, and the reporter being led around by whatever the subject wants to say. I approached the story determined to write it my way. As a writer, you must be *active* and make your own defensible, fact-based decisions about the structure of a piece. You must locate a theme, organize the narrative as *you decide,* and provide transitions and verities so the reader can follow your progression of thought.

After interviewing Barry and completing the profile, "Barry's Way," I felt a sense of purpose that had previously eluded me as a writer. As his story came into focus, I discovered my own chief aim: to document metaphysical experience in history and practice. I had framed Barry as an exhibit of positive-mind principles, which is exactly what could be gleaned from his career and training, if one knew where to look. (I've repeatedly had "breaks" as a historian and journalist, such as discovering occult literary influences in the speeches of Ronald Reagan, which I've written about in the *Washington Post* and *Salon;* this is not because I just happened upon revealing material but because I *recognized* terminology, references, and phrases that are missed by most mainstream historians and journalists, who have no background in the esoteric or spiritual.*)

---

*E.g., see my article "Reagan and the Occult," *Washington Post,* April 30, 2010.

About two weeks after my article appeared in October 2003, I got a phone call, wholly unexpectedly, from Barry's father, Joe, whom I had never met. He loved the story. *"Mitch,"* he growled into the phone, *"you stick with this thing!"* He meant my writing about metaphysical ideas. Joe had no idea of my struggle and my past; he didn't know me. But he *got it,* dead on. He saw what I was after, and his drill-sergeant encouragement gave me just the lift I needed. Barry later told me that Joe, who died in 2013, had played that role in several people's lives.

I experienced the renewal of my wish to be a writer—but on terms that far better suited my interests and temperament. I felt a sense of mission and purpose—and I acted on it. About three years from the day I heard from Joe Zito, I had a contract from Bantam for my first book, *Occult America,* which won a 2010 PEN Oakland literary award (the *New York Times* called it "The 'Blue-Collar' PEN"), received widespread and positive reviews, got endorsements from figures as diffuse as Ken Burns and Deepak Chopra, and resulted in my appearances on *CBS Sunday Morning, Dateline NBC,* NPR's *All Things Considered,* among other national shows. In the years ahead, my writing on alternative spiritual topics ran in the *New York Times,* the *Wall Street Journal,* the *Washington Post,* and many other national publications. I had left a regional newspaper with my head down at age twenty-two. By my forties, I was seriously and unexpectedly back in the game.

The road was gradual but perceptible, helped at a sudden moment by an opportunity for which I was prepared. We're often told that you should never give up on your dreams, and I agree with that—*but at the same time your dreams must not be idle or fantastical, and they must employ powers that are within your reach.* Resilience is an act. The constituent elements of a thing must be in place, and in action, before its realization.

Here's another example of positive-mind mechanics from the sports world; it reinforces the importance of writing down a goal. *Sports Illustrated* named Cornell University wrestling champion Kyle Dake as its college athlete of the year in 2013. The collegian told a reporter how he built his career on arduous training and New Thought methods (he didn't use that term, but few do). For three-and-a-half years, the wrestler filled a red-covered spiral notebook with 2,978 affirmations, written at night and in the morning, affirming his desired weight-class victories during the course of four wrestling seasons.

Sports Illustrated put it this way:

> Once in the morning and once at night as a freshman Dake wrote, 2010 141 lb DI NCAA National Champion. Twice in the morning and twice at night as a sophomore he wrote, 2011 149 lb DI National Champion. Thrice in the morning and thrice at night as a junior he wrote, 2012 157 lb DI National Champion. Four times in the morning and four times at night as a senior he wrote, 2013 165 lb DI National Champion.

On March 23, 2013, Kyle Dake made history as the first college wrestler to win an NCAA title in four different weight classes.

Athletics provide a useful window on New Thought because not only do many Olympians, collegians, and pros use visualizations and affirmations (this is true for dozens with whom I've spoken—the U.S. Olympic swim team has employed its own visualization coach), but the results are chartable. My younger son's gymnastics coach requires team members to a carry a notebook with them and write down a goal for each day's practice. And, of course, myriad factors, including natural talent and ceaseless training, must be present.

WHAT ABOUT MONEY?

I have earned financial rewards from my work, and I wish the same for everyone reading these words. But I must add that discovering where your dreams and abilities intersect is no guarantee of earning a living. This book is not an employment guide. It is a guide to using the energies of your mind in the direction of meaning, purpose, and self-expression—to not die with the words "what if?" on your lips. Becoming an actor, for example, may not lead to a steady paycheck—you may need to forever retain your day job. But failing to fulfill a creative role may otherwise leave a tragic gap in your life.

As a teen, I dreamed of being a professional actor (something you may have gleaned from my examples). I attended the Long Island High School for the Arts, a regional equivalent of New York's High School of the Performing Arts, the school dramatized in *Fame*. At age sixteen, however, I let go of this dream. Given the rifts in my home, and the financial disaster that accompanied it, I felt that I needed to plan for a reliable career. With thoughts of a steady future, I threw myself into more traditional studies. Wearing used clothes and hauling junk to a penny-a-pound recycling center, I was determined to be *practical*.

Many years later, self-satisfied with my decision, I sometimes judged other people who remained dedicated to acting but who, as their thirties wore on, seemed to have little chance of earning a living at it. I once told a friend of mine, an outstanding but struggling stage actor, that, as I saw it, if someone hadn't broken through by his or her mid-thirties, it was time to embark on Plan B, and seek a different career path.

My friend disagreed. "If acting is an art that someone is dedicated to," he said, "he should stick with it. That's what an artist does—that's who they are." He was right. In my "realism" I had forgotten that life is about more than settling or being practical—it is about being expressive of something, of standing for something. For all those years, I realized, I was mistaken in my attitude, if not my decision. There is potency and aliveness in pursuing your art—even when it doesn't pay the rent by itself, or at all. "A lot of great artists and musicians have day jobs all their lives," a musician friend, Mel Bergman, told me.

Mel is a visionary maker of specialty guitars, including the Wheely, a custom guitar for people who use wheelchairs. He also plays in the pioneering instrumental surf-rock band The Phantom Surfers. "That's great!" I told him upon first hearing of his surf-instrumental genre.

"That's what everyone says," he replied. "Everyone says it's great—no one listens to it."

He wasn't being cynical; he was just reflecting the financial reality facing many artists. We all want to arrive at a place where our art and passions, whatever they are, eventually become our dedicated job, and hopefully support a gainful lifestyle. I take that very seriously. But that, in the end, is not the true measurement of achievement. Pursuing your personal agencies, engaging in the creative act, and enabling the highest experiences of others, in whatever form, is the only lasting measure of success. It begins with one absolutely dedicated goal.

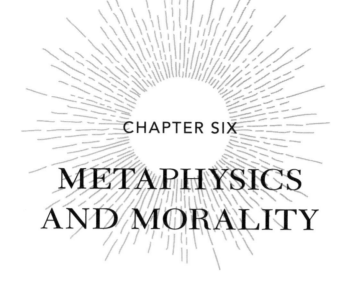

CHAPTER SIX

METAPHYSICS AND MORALITY

Man's imagination is the man himself, and the world as imagination sees it is the real world, but it is our duty to imagine all that is lovely and of good report.

NEVILLE, *OUT OF THIS WORLD*

When I was a child, the rabbi of our local synagogue in Queens started wearing a toupee. Some judged him for it, arguing that a spiritual leader should model self-acceptance and teach that life's highest values are unseen. One of my family members, in a crushingly embarrassing moment, confronted him about it on a greeting line one Saturday after services.

"Don't you think that's a little ridiculous?" she said.

"I don't think that's any of your affair," he responded through tight lips.

The rabbi was correct—not just about the confrontation but also about his choice. His detractors were wrong.

I am adamant that there is absolutely nothing wrong with the pursuit of beauty, as you personally conceive it, and with the endeavor to reform the outer world, including your own physicality, to your mind's-eye image of the good.

Do you blanche at that and insist that the spiritual path is one of inner growth and radical personal acceptance? I say the spiritual path is to make you into a vessel for the highest ideals of creativity and productivity, as pertaining to your lived experience. An athlete must be strong and fast; a dancer svelte and elegant; an actor suited to his role. There are, of course, personal limits. Our bodies and minds decay, and if there is a higher form of life than the physical, then we must bow to it and seek glimpses of it in our lived experience. But *those facts in themselves* do not serve to deny an individual, any more than an artist or entrepreneur, the measured pursuit of his or her ideal. We live in two worlds. To deny one for the other brings us no closer to truth.

Indeed, concern with personal appearance, as with money, is something from which no one is free. We are created as physical beings. Look at the emphasis on beauty throughout the great cultures: the ornate ceremonial garbs of the Hebrews and the Maya; the tributes to physicality in Vedic, Greek, and Roman art; and the sensuality of the Kama Sutra and Song of Solomon. All forms of personal existence other than the sensory are speculative, however much we hold to them as ideals.

At the same time, I am keenly aware of the danger of one-sidedness with regard to physicality, as with other matters of life. When physical development and outer aesthetics become not just a value but an ultimate end, not just a temporal aspect of self-expression but an absolute in themselves, we cross into ethically dangerous ground. When concern with appearance grows obsessive, when it becomes a god rather than an aspect of the individual as a reflection of God, we are lost.

Balance, not strained asceticism, is the key.

To that end, and to avoid the pitfalls of one-sidedness, don't dare begin a program of mental metaphysics without having a well-rounded ethical philosophy as a daily guide. Whether it's the Gospels, the Ethics of the Fathers from the Talmud, the Bhagavad Gita—you must have a perennial work of religious or ethical philosophy to serve as a set of personal guardrails, or you may fall into a trap of selfishness and narrow pursuit of goodies.

I have had the experience myself. Mind metaphysics can direct us toward manipulative and harmful paths and persuade us that the mere *wanting* of something is validation enough, and that the pursuit of any desire, regardless of who it affects or what network of forces it instigates, is justifiable. That is false—and the ethical traditions of the world tell us so.

At the same time, let no one else dictate to you what you should want. Or what form your wants should take. A financier once said to me: "What good is something unless you can put your name on it?" I find that statement coarse and shallow. It reduces all of life to possession. And yet, I challenge "spiritual" people to think for a moment before flat out dismissing it. Unless you possess utter certainty of an unseen world and of a higher scale of values—not as voiced by someone else but as lived by you—it may be worth allowing yourself to be peripherally haunted by that statement, which raises the possibility that the world we see really is all there is. Now, I believe that the physical world is not all there is. There is an unseen world. But—and mark this—that belief itself cannot function as an excuse not to excel in this one. Many people, especially in the alternative spiritual culture, adopt "spirituality" as an escape hatch from the demands and requirements of outer life. Pause carefully before you tell yourself or another that you hold a different, and presumably better, scale of values than those found in outward strivings.

The financier's statement, however ugly, captured half a truth. The whole truth is that our lives, as vessels for the Higher and receptors of thought, are indelibly bound up with the world and circumstances in which we find ourselves. Whatever higher influences we feel, and great thoughts we think or are experienced by us through the influence of others, are like heat dissipated in the vacuum of space unless those thoughts are directed into a structure or receptacle, whether physical, material, or in the form of personal conduct. Thought not acted upon is like an echo whose vibratory power quickly weakens and fades. This is a good thing regarding thoughts that are irrational or harmful, which, if quickly dissipated, impair neither our psychology nor physiology. But when constructive thoughts are allowed to die, or whither through neglect, the results are tragic. We cannot and will never feel complete without building the stages and structures that are representative of our ideas and proper to our needs.

Think of someone who professes a vision that is not enacted—who thinks himself capable of enactment, and who often dies in that belief, without realizing that ability is never abstract. It is in application or it is nothing. Few things are more impotent than someone standing before a minimalist painting in an art museum and saying derisively, "I could do that." He could not and, more so, he will not; he will never make the attempt, which would at least demonstrate to him how demanding an act of creation really is. Never allow that to be you.

In a passage from *The Prince,* Machiavelli identified three kinds of intellect: the first is the intellect that can do the thing itself, which he deemed excellent; the second kind of intellect can judge the thing, which he called good; the third can neither do nor judge, which he considered completely worthless. At our best, we are made to act. It is agony to live otherwise, quiet agony, perhaps, but the kind that fuels chronic reliance on gossip, food, booze, or other compulsions and means of escapism, which mark off the years of our lives. Action is intrinsic to happiness and self-possession. In his 1841 essay "History," Emerson observed that if you were to relocate Napoleon to surroundings that disallowed action, everything exceptional about him would vanish:

Put Napoleon in an island prison, let his faculties find no men to act on, no Alps to climb, no stake to play for, and he would beat the air and appear stupid. Transport him to large countries, dense population, complex interests, and antagonist power, and you shall see that the man Napoleon, bounded, that is, by such a profile and outline, is not the virtual Napoleon.

You must act on your constructive thoughts. This requires being around people who are capable of supporting your aims and avoiding those who deter them. You must also have an aim that is sustaining rather than withering, a point to which we now turn.

THE GOOD WISH

We all know the story of King Midas—or think we do. Owed a favor by the god Dionysus, the covetous ruler asks that everything he touch turn to gold. Dionysus, realizing that it could lead to ruin, reluctantly grants the king's wish. Midas soon finds himself unable even to eat as his food turns to gold. In a nineteenth-century retelling by American writer Nathaniel Hawthorne, the king embraces his daughter only to turn her into gold. Midas realizes that he has sacrificed life and love for riches. In the Greek myth, the agonized ruler prays to Dionysus for mercy and the god tells him to wash himself in a river, whose waters absorb his "gift," and turn the pale yellow of gold. The curse is lifted. Midas, despising riches, lives out the rest of his life in the woods.

Like Midas, the greatest challenge we face is what to serve—what to dedicate ourselves to. The Gospels tell us that we cannot serve dual aims: "No man can serve two masters: for either he will hate the one, and love the other; or else he will hold to the one, and despise the other" (Matthew 6:24).

Years ago, I knew a brilliant man, a true seeker, who was divided between pursuing his spiritual search and his studies as a physician. He felt torn and unsure of what to do. He then grasped the passage from Matthew 6:33: "But seek ye first the kingdom of God, and His righteousness; and all these things shall be added unto you." He had found his answer. Nothing in his inner search meant sacrificing his medical education. He was simply being guided to "seek first" the kingdom of heaven—and then all else, including medical degrees and training, would be added. His setting of priorities did not mean truncating his existence. He eventually received his degree from Harvard Medical

School and went on to practice as a physician, including at a community clinic in Harlem. He did not sacrifice medicine. But his *first* priority was his spiritual search. And he was a brilliant spiritual teacher (although he didn't want to be called a teacher), without whose influence I would not be writing these words.

How can we understand how to set priorities in a world that bombards us with activities and possibilities? Unlike ancient men and women, whose social roles were highly stratified and whose lives were largely dictated by birth, geography, and background, we modern Westerners face an incredibly tantalizing array of choices and consumer temptations. Even if we consider ourselves spiritual, we are not hermits, monks, or contemplatives. We are people of the world. So, accepting that work, family, commerce, and outer activities will necessarily consume part of our lives, how do we follow the precept to "seek first" God and the kingdom? Obadiah Harris, president of the University of Philosophical Research in Los Angeles, offers a guidepost in his manuscript and forthcoming book *The Aim of Life:*

> All motivation for action should come from the Divine. Whenever we are prompted to act we should first refer the action to God. We should ask ourselves whether the contemplated action leaves us quiet and composed, or whether the mere thought of it throws us in a turmoil of worry and distraction. If it has the latter disturbing effect, it is not Divinely inspired or directed. Any action that does not proceed out of inner peace and silence cannot have the right spiritual base.

This principle does not ask too much of us—it meets us where we live. Does the action under consideration leave us "quiet and composed," or does its prospect throw us into "worry and distraction"? We may ignore the "worry and distraction" in hopes of receiving some trophy or reward that makes it worthwhile; but we cannot claim that we lack the necessary perceptual ability or contemplative skills to acknowledge and work toward the principle that Harris offers us.

In considering his principle, I am reminded of another from Carlos Castaneda's 1968 book, *The Teachings of Don Juan*. Forget, for a moment, about the controversies surrounding Castaneda—we all know them. But his book, for me, offers splendid insights, and it left an impression on me as a child, when my sister first brought it home. The figure of Don Juan tells Carlos:

> Look at every path closely and deliberately. Try it as many times as you think necessary. Then ask yourself, and yourself alone, one question. This question is one that only a very old man asks. My benefactor told me about it once when I was young, and my blood was too vigorous for me to understand it. Now I do understand it. I will tell you what it is: Does this path have a heart? All paths are the same: they lead nowhere. They are paths going through the bush, or into the bush. In my life I could say I have traversed long, long paths, but I am not anywhere. My benefactor's question has meaning now. Does this path have a heart? If it does, the path is good; if it doesn't, it is of no use. Both paths lead nowhere; but one has a heart, the other doesn't. One makes for a joyful journey; as long as you follow it, you are one with it. The other will make you curse your life. One makes you strong; the other weakens you.

THE POWER OF SERVICE

Usually—and note this very carefully—a realistic and healthful goal comports with some sense of higher good and can be described in plain terms for how it improves the lives of others. Fantasies tend to run in selfish directions; whereas service tends toward discipline.

By service, I do not mean something dreary or self-sacrificing. I have ambitions of my own as a writer and speaker; but I also harbor and act on the hope that what I produce gives people better ways of thinking and reasoning, especially in areas of our culture where critical thought is in short supply. I have turned down opportunities to host or appear on TV shows because I was asked either to promulgate conspiracy theories or to enlist people into questionable practices, such as using a Ouija board to reach deceased loved ones. So, when I say that I believe my work, whatever its flaws, must impart some benefit, and I define that as helping people to think more clearly and engage more civilly, I'm not attempting to say something pretty about myself, but I have rejected enticing offers that did not hold to that aim.

In my twenty-plus years of experience as a publisher—and I think many of my fellow editors would agree with this—I have experienced few things more depleting than working with an author who wants to succeed more than he wants to serve something clarifying and good. Industriousness is a virtue. Narrow ambition is not. Nor is greed. Or the ravenous hunger to be celebrated or validated. A narrowly conceived or obsessively self-serving wish renders a person into someone who is constantly draining other people—of resources, of emotions, of money, of energies. It is taxing and even physically unhealthy to be around someone whose wish for adulation, influence, or riches severs him or her from purpose.

I'm not saying that driving ambition is wrong. Without the drive to attain, bridges would never get built, cures would never get discovered, the surface of the moon never walked. But when the drive to attain becomes one's chief quality—when it surpasses all other purpose—that's when bridges fall down, because graft overcomes workmanship. Graft is sometimes described, or used to be, as "selling out." Selling out means: putting money before quality. There is no other definition.

I've had the privilege of publishing filmmaker David Lynch, creator of *Twin Peaks* and movies including *Mulholland Drive* and *Blue Velvet*. He is often credited with bridging the gap between independent art-house films and Hollywood moviemaking. People respect David, and he is a hero to many film students and young artists. It's because he has never sold out. David's genius as a director is that he is entirely, even virtuosically, capable of writing and shooting a standard thriller; but he takes that ability and zigzags with it, so that his movies and television shows are a combination of suspenseful storytelling and surrealistic dreamscapes. He doesn't set out to make a statement, or to make a killing. He simply honors the idea. Fulfilling the idea is his highest ethic.

In my favorite of David's movies, *Mulholland Drive,* there occurs a scene where a mysterious character called "The Cowboy" expounds on life to a cynical young Hollywood director, Adam Kesher. Consider a piece of that scene:

COWBOY: Man's attitude, man's attitude goes some ways, the way his life will be. Is that something you might agree with?

ADAM: Sure.

COWBOY: Now, did you answer because that's what you thought I wanted to hear, or did you think about what I said, and answer cause you truly believe that to be right?

ADAM: I agree with what you said. Truly.

COWBOY: What I say?

ADAM: That a man's attitude determines to a large extent how his life will be.

COWBOY: So, since you agree, you must be a person who does not care about the good life.

ADAM: How's that?

COWBOY: Well, stop for a little second; think about it. Can you do that for me?

ADAM: (laughs) Okay, I'm thinking.

COWBOY: No, you're not thinking. You're too busy being a smart aleck to be thinking. Now, I want you to think, and stop being a smart aleck. Can you try that for me?

In fall 2016 I interviewed David for the public radio show *Interfaith Voices,* and we discussed that scene:

Mitch: Now, personally speaking, I find a whole philosophy of life in that scene. I think if we lived on another planet and had no information about life except for this scene, and this was all that reached us, we would make it. We would find a way to make it. What The Cowboy says informs a lot of the work that I'm doing right now about the power of thought. How do you view the power of an attitude, and do you think we're all too busy being smart alecks?

David: Well, there's a lot of smart aleck stuff going on these days, but, the thing is, the key is, Mitch, you can talk about people changing their attitudes and you can make laws that kinda indicate what a good attitude is, and you should have that. But the thing is that the torment and the beliefs and the way are inside the people. And you can't change that unless you get down on a deeper level and you gotta get underneath the problem, Einstein said, in order to solve the problem. You can't get deeper than the unified field, that transcendent, the ocean of pure consciousness, the being. So you teach people Transcendental Meditation. All this negativity flies out, all the gold comes in and attitudes change, but it's not because of some law or somebody telling you to change your attitude, it's natural. It just changes. And people don't, for instance, feel like blowing someone's head off anymore, they just don't want to do that anymore. They don't wanna rob any bank, they don't wanna beat their wife. You know, they might have enjoyed beating their wife last week, but now they don't wanna do that anymore.

Part of what David is driving at, I think, is that a person cannot be detached from the larger whole, whether you call it the unified field or by another term. A go-it-alone approach is synonymous with destruction.

In the vein of David's career, I would add one more observation: Being self-directed and working with integrity makes you magnetic and attractive to people. While everyone else is trying to curry favor, the person with integrity and purpose stands out—and stands *for* something. Take note of this passage from Ralph Waldo Emerson's "Powers and Laws of Thought":

> Let me whisper a secret; nobody ever forgives any admiration in you of them, any overestimate of what they do or have. I acquiesce to be that I am, but I wish no one to be civil to me. Strong men understand this very well. Power fraternizes with power, and wishes you not to be like him but like yourself. Echo the leaders and they will fast enough see that you have nothing for them. They came to you for something they had not. There is always a loss of truth and power when a man leaves working for himself to work for another. Absolutely speaking, I can only work for myself. All my good is magnetic, and I educate not by lessons but by going about my business.

Seen from a certain perspective, the "golden touch" is integrity. If people grant us favors, it is not because we kowtow to them, but because we supply something from within ourselves to which others are naturally drawn; it is often in the form of a steadfastness, a willingness to do what is right by our own lights, and to shoulder the consequences.

People talk big—but few are willing to deal with consequences. I once published an author whose book was in danger of cancelation due to chronic lateness. He dodged my calls, and when I finally caught up with him to explain the situation, he protested: "I finish what I start." That was beside the point. He was already at liberty to do what he wanted, either finish or not finish. But he could not demand that someone still had to pay his way, and on his terms. (I actually did give him a break and readjusted his schedule. He never delivered.)

Courage is something you must do all by yourself. If you go your own way, you may have to face an occasional loss. But you cannot call yourself courageous while also insisting that others, regardless of their needs, pay or service you, when and how much you want. I often tell people: don't act the part of the hero *after* you cash the check. Know what you're getting into and make it clear whether you are on board with what's being asked of you, including in matters of time, quantity, and schedule. Capitalist philosopher Ayn Rand calls this "the sanctity of contract"—it is your word. It is your life itself. You can't save the world, or contribute anything of value to the world, if you cannot, as a moral baseline, keep your word and commitments.

And if you face a loss, perhaps by turning down a profitable but poorly timed or distasteful assignment, consider what you gain: the reward of sustaining your vision and the honor of your peers. I have observed in such cases that equal or better opportunities often arrive, almost with uncanny proximity to the one you rejected. We are defined by what we agree to as much as by what we reject.

GOD AND SALESMAN

There is no division between good commerce and personal goodness. In fact, we often learn about one from pursuing the other. A close friend, Liam O'Malley, once told me: "America is the only nation where a guide to salesmanship can lead a person to a search for God." His observation is absolutely correct. Cynics will never understand why.

When a person begins to probe quality self-help or motivational literature, particularly books on using mental therapeutics for success, he or she inevitably begins to ask questions about the underlying laws and forces of life.

I have argued that not everything that happens to us is under the workings of the mind. We live under myriad laws and forces, including physical limitations, twists of fortune, and accidents. But part of what happens to us—perhaps the most significant part—emerges from the workings of our minds, emotions, and sense of self. When someone acknowledges that unseen antecedents lie behind the outer events of life (which is, in a sense, the key insight of modern thought—in psychology, economics, and the sciences), he also begins to ponder the existence and role of immaterial causes.

If universal laws and ethics exist, then it follows that at least part of what happens to us in life is rooted not only in attitudes, decisions, and insights, but in something more: If thought has a nonphysical component, whether in the form of some kind of anomalous transfer of communication between two minds, or the elusive capacity of an observation or conviction to influence body and circumstance, then we start to approach the question of a metaphysical dimension to life.

Indeed, if anomalous forms of communication can be demonstrated, or at least sustained as a reasonable question in a laboratory setting, it opens us to the possibility that the mind operates not only within the gray matter of the brain, but also within a nonphysical field of activity—that our thoughts, and those of others, are part of a creative agency outside of commonly observed sensory data.

If we surmise, or at least consider, that collective humanity participates in an immaterial intelligence, this begs the question of the existence of what Ralph Waldo Emerson termed an "Over-Soul" and Napoleon Hill called the "Master Mind"—a quality of intelligence that is greater than our individualized thoughts. The question of nonphysical intelligence leads also to the consideration of a Higher Power, or God.

The reader of almost any motivational or success-oriented book has urgent earthly needs, often financial. But the dedicated seeker—the person whose questions are persistent and ever deepening—will inevitably find that the quest for a "better way" in material affairs broadens to include the meaning and nature of all of life. The sincere search for a "better way" leads to questions of purpose and existence.

We "cannot serve God and mammon," Scripture tells us. But a life of seeking may lead you to a different kind of relationship with mammon, and to questions of how to make mammon a servant rather than a master (whether in circumstances of plenty or lack), as well as to what mammon is really *for*. These questions in themselves direct the striving individual to consider how his or her personal aim relates to, or results from, a higher principle of life.

My friend Liam, who I quoted above, is a case in point. He is a gifted and passionate musician, an accomplished salesman and marketer, and a dedicated seeker—his life is a crossroads of the search for God and the question of how to live rightly in the world. Liam is someone for whom money, ethics, and seeking are one and the same. There is no "inner" or "outer." It's all *one life*.

In this vein of thought, I wrote the following "Prayer for Salesmen"—celebrating the seen and the unseen in the lives of these overlooked heroes of American commerce:

> You are the salesman. You are the foundation of human commerce.
> You are the salesman. Without you, no services or inventions would
> reach those who need them.
> No homes would change hands.
> No safety or security would be had through the issuance of
> insurance and sound financial plans.
> Products and advances would stagnate.
> Inventors, doctors, financiers, police, and peacemakers would not
> know how to find the tools they need—or help others use what
> they offer.
> Who praises your work? You are unseen by the scholar, the social
> critic, and the artist.
> But you support them.
> You send your children and loved ones to their schools and galleries.
> You sell their books and make their beautiful things available.
> You are the salesman. The person of commerce and service, who
> makes so much possible in our world.
> Contracts and selling appear in some of the earliest human
> documents. Your work is sacred.

You are the salesman. You suffer a thousand "no's" with patience
    until you discover that one person who needs what you offer.
You are never bitter. You cannot be.
You are the salesman. The one on whom all commerce depends.
This hour we think of you: We pray for your success; we thank you
    for your forbearance; we ask God's blessings on you and those
    you support.
You are the salesman. Never give up. We need you.

THE STRENGTH OF VIRTUE

New Thought methods can be used for generative or destructive ends.
In general, though not always explicitly, New Thought writers have
relied upon Scriptural ethics. This is why New Thought philosophy
surpasses the morality—though rarely the intellectual excellence—of
figures such as Aleister Crowley and other purveyors of ceremonial
magick and the metaphysical search for power.

The important thing to bear in mind when experimenting with
mind-power methods is that we are not adrift in an ethical ocean. If
Scripture and other ancient sacred works supply us with hints of man's
creative potential, we are also supplied with safety ropes. As noted, the
ethics of manifestation must be married to some version of Gospel ethics, or to put it in simplest terms: the Golden Rule.

That can induce eye rolling. The ethic of "doing unto others" is
so familiar that we think of it as a nursery-school lesson, or see it as a
tedious truism like "early to bed, early to rise," with no insight for serious people. Yet there is an unseen dimension to the Golden Rule, which,
when you realize it, is so powerful that you will receive an entirely new
assessment of your life.

In the months before I began this book, I felt that an unnamed
something was curtailing my progress toward my aims. Something was
diverting my ability to envision and pursue higher possibilities for
myself and others. I was stuck in a holding pattern.

I found the answer to my predicament in a passage from Napoleon Hill's 1928 multivolume work *The Law of Success,* which is, in my view, the greatest thing he ever wrote (though it is surpassed in popularity by his better-known *Think and Grow Rich*). The key to my problem, I learned from Hill, was the Golden Rule. Bear in mind that the precept "do unto others as you would have them do unto you" appears in virtually every religious and ethical teaching across cultures and time, from the Vedas to the Tao Te Ching to the meditations of Marcus Aurelius. It was dubbed the Golden Rule in late seventeenth-century England and is now as familiar as "have a nice day." But the Golden Rule contains an inner truth.

Using modern terms, Hill related the Golden Rule to the phenomenon of autosuggestion, or the suggestions we continually make to ourselves. Autosuggestion was the tool identified by French mind theorist Émile Coué; it is the basis for Coué's "day by day" mantra and is the psychological mechanism in back of many of today's placebo studies. The core principle of autosuggestion is that what you believe and internally repeat takes root in your intellect and emotions, shaping your subconscious perceptions of self and the surrounding world. I think this process has been so widely demonstrated that it surpasses theory and can be understood as impactful and determinative fact.

But take careful note of Hill's insight that the autosuggestive process is also triggered by *what you think about others.*

"Your thoughts of others are registered in your subconscious mind through the principle of autosuggestion," Hill wrote, "thereby building your own character in exact duplicate." Hence: "You must *'think of others as you wish them to think of you.'* The law upon which the Golden Rule is based begins affecting you, for good or evil, the moment you release a *thought.*" It is worth considering Hill's point of view at length:

If all your acts toward others, and even your thoughts of others, are registered in your subconscious mind, through the principle of autosuggestion, thereby building your own character in exact duplicate of your thoughts and acts, can you not see how important it is to guard those acts and thoughts?

We are now in the very heart of the real reason for doing unto others as we would have them do unto us, for it is obvious that whatever we do unto others we do unto ourselves.

Stated in another way, every act and every thought you release modifies your own character in exact conformity with the nature of the act or thought, and your character is a sort of center of magnetic attraction, which attracts to you the people and conditions that harmonize with it. You cannot indulge in an act toward another person without having first created the nature of that act in your own thought, and you cannot release a thought without planting the sum and substance and nature of it in your own subconscious mind, there to become a part and parcel of your own character.

Grasp this simple principle and you will understand why you cannot afford to hate or envy another person. You will also understand why you cannot afford to strike back, in kind, at those who do you an injustice. Likewise, you will understand the injunction, "Return good for evil."

When you indulge in fantasies of revenge, such as telling others off or score settling—which, frankly, make up an alarming amount of my passive or associative thoughts—you not only shackle yourself to past wrongs, but also to the wrongs that you would do in exchange. Your acts of violation toward another, whether by mind, talk, emotion, or hand, reenact themselves in your psyche and perceptions. You are lowered to the level of people you resent or even hate when you counter—mentally or otherwise—their type of behavior. An adjunct to the Golden Rule could be: *You become what you do not forgive.*

Conversely, thoughts of forgiveness—is there any more noble a thought?—add a special solidity to your character, which manifests as self-respect, self-possession, and, as it happens, greater personal effectiveness. If you find it difficult to enact generous or forgiving thoughts, you can arrive at them indirectly by abstaining from gossip. Acts of gossiping, tale bearing, and spreading or listening to rumors are a smog that clouds your experience and intellect as much as the lives of those who are defamed. An enormous amount of our interactions, and social media intake, are based in gossip. You will discover that every act of abstaining from gossip or rumor, even some of the time (perfection is a depleting target), innately brings out your nobler leanings and bestows upon you a new self-confidence.

We often justify tales of malice or character smearing by claiming that we're merely telling the truth. That is false. Virtually every bit of hearsay to which we listen, promulgate, or repeat is false, half true, or mitigated by gravely serious circumstances of which we are unaware. We often engage in such things to relive boredom or make ourselves more interesting to others. We fear that without gossiping we will be uninteresting to friends and workmates. This cements us into a cycle of violating our best interests and intentions, and often attaches us to people who are depleting rather than supportive. And, rest assured, your suspicion that your gossip mates are also talking about you is correct. Cut the cord.

The ancients echoed this point of view. In a manuscript that has come down to us only in fragments, the Greek playwright Euripides cautioned to respect your neighbor's privacy: "Zeus hates busybodies." In Judaism no sin other than murder is considered more serious than tale bearing or *lashon hara,* Hebrew for "evil tongue." As a child, I'll never forget the experience of hearing a young rabbi tell a youth congregation that only the sin of murder is graver than gossip. "There's no joke about it," he said steadily. Never have I witnessed a roomful of rowdy kids so stilled into silence. The rabbi was not scaring us but impressing us with a hallowed truth. In forty years, I've never forgotten it, though I have failed at it. New Thought, based in Scriptural ethics, offers a similar, subtly equivalent prohibition: "What man says of others will be said of him," wrote Florence Scovel Shinn. The act of slaying another's reputation is a moral suicide, Neville Goddard taught, noting that thought concretizes reality for the speaker as much as for the one spoken of.

In sum, your thoughts about yourself *and about others* can be likened to an invisible engine that molds your own character and experience. If you find yourself bumping against limits, or having difficulty formulating or carrying out an aim, reconsider your relationship to the Golden Rule and gossip. You may be surprised by the onrush of creativity you experience when abstaining from gossip. An elusive goal, an unfinished idea, or a sought-after relationship may take shape before you.

CHAPTER SEVEN

WORKING CLASS MYSTIC

The Example of James Allen

How can we put these ideas into action? In the epigraph of this book, I quoted Emerson saying that metaphysics must be biography. The best example I know of metaphysical principle as biography appears in the life of early twentieth-century British writer and New Thought devotee, James Allen. If Allen's name is unfamiliar, you probably know his short, meditative book *As a Man Thinketh,* which has been read by millions, and has shaped the culture of self-help since it appeared in 1903.

Allen epitomized the dimensions and power of thought to transform a life. He joined New Thought ambitions to social idealism, as a supporter of labor rights, an early advocate for the humane treatment of animals and vegetarianism, a Christian ethicist, and a mystic seeker. Allen's life was his greatest creation.

His literary career was short, ranging roughly from the publication of his first book in 1901 to his death in 1912. Yet in those eleven years Allen completed nineteen books, some of them published posthumously. In the same year that he produced *As a Man Thinketh,* 1903, Allen put out another book—less known but equally powerful in scope and practicality: *All These Things Added.*

In *All These Things Added,* he prescribed a formula of day-to-day living intended to bring personal fulfillment and higher realization. Like the physician-teacher I wrote about in the previous chapter, Allen based his outlook on Matthew 6:33: "But seek ye first the kingdom of God, and his righteousness; and all these things shall be added unto you."

The book captured Allen's struggle to live in the awareness that we experience a broadened, more bountiful existence when we attempt to serve something higher than ourselves; when we strive to create something—a work of writing, an invention, a new law, a reversal of injustice—that is lasting, beneficial, serviceable, and equal to the claims made for it.

In the book's most memorable passage, Allen reflects on the feeding habits of birds—and how they resemble the consumptive patterns of human beings. He recalls his experience of feeding birds and noticing that the more food he gave them—he once tossed a full loaf of bread—the more frenzied their behavior. "It is not scarcity that produces competition," he concludes, *"it is abundance."*

I'm not sure that his point is entirely right. Scarcity produces its own form of ruthlessness and even horror, a truth seen in conflicts around the world and explored with unflinching honesty in Cormac McCarthy's novel *The Road.* But Allen's greater point, and the lesson I take from his observation, is that abundance doesn't sate hunger or competition. Abundance, in its grossest form, when not wed to labor, tends to leave us unsatisfied, petty, grasping, and covetous.

I have visited and spoken at "leisure villages" for wealthy or well-off retirees and been shocked to discover that, amid material profusion and hours of down time, there often prevails an atmosphere of sniping and finickiness, as among spoiled children.

The noblest aspects of human nature emerge when the individual is striving toward something. When the thing striven for is attained, however, such as a comfortable and prosperous old age, the human mind often redirects its attention onto the smallest and most fleeting details of quotidian life. Abundance can be a kind of slavery insofar as it feeds and foments what might be called "it"—the lowest self within us that feeds on habit, consumption, and routine.

James Allen, by contrast, was compelled to struggle most of his life. But that struggle never deformed him. The decisive factor in his life—the thing that kept him from lapsing into pettiness or malaise— was that he saw life's upward hill not as a path toward comfort but toward refinement. He believed that human growth, if it occurred at all, emerged from an ever-advancing pursuit of inner repose, simplicity of habit, and reduction of wants. The historical details of Allen's life demonstrate this.

METAPHYSICS THE HARD WAY

James Allen was born on November 28, 1864, to a working-class family in the industrial town of Leicester, in central England. His mother, Martha, could neither read nor write. (She signed her marriage certificate with an *X*.) His father, William, was the proprietor of a knitting factory. The eldest of three brothers, James was bookish and mild, doted upon by his father, who treasured learning and reading. He vowed to make "young Jim" into a scholar.

When James turned fifteen, central England's textile industry experienced a severe slump, and William lost his business. In 1879, he pulled together his savings and traveled alone to America, hoping to find work, reestablish himself, and then bring over the rest of the family. But on the brink of the Christmas season, the unthinkable occurred. Two days after William reached New York City, news returned home that he had been killed—the victim of a murder-robbery. William's body, its pockets picked over, lay in a city hospital.

The Allen family faced economic disaster. James, the studious teen, was forced to leave school and find work locally as a factory framework knitter to support his mother and two brothers. He sometimes put in fifteen-hour days. The job consumed him for nine years.

Even amid the strains of factory life, however, James retained his father's love for literature, and whenever possible he read Scripture, Shakespeare, Western translations of Buddhism, and early tracts on vegetarianism and animal rights. His interest in the ethical treatment of animals grew from his studies of karma and Buddhism. Allen retained the self-possessed, serious bearing that his father had sought to cultivate in him. When his workmates went out drinking or caught up on sleep Allen studied and read two to three hours a day. Coworkers called him "the Saint" and "the Parson."

Around 1889, Allen found new employment in London as a private secretary and stationer, presumably friendlier vocations to the genteel, self-educated man than factory work. The move to London, and the access it gave him to lending libraries and bookstores, marked a turning point in his life. Over the next decade, Allen cultivated an interest in the world's spiritual philosophies, poring over the works of John Milton, Ralph Waldo Emerson, Walt Whitman, and translations of the Bhagavad Gita, Tao Te Ching, and the sayings of Buddha.

Later on, he grew interested in America's burgeoning New Thought culture through the work of Ralph Waldo Trine, Christian D. Larson, and Orison Swett Marden. He developed a personal philosophy that closely aligned with New Thought. The mind, as Allen saw it, is an organ through which God and man coalesce; as such, thoughts determine destiny.

Also in London, he met his wife and intellectual partner, Lily Oram. They wed in 1895, and the following year gave birth to a daughter, Nora, their only child.

By 1898, Allen discovered an outlet for his spiritual and social interests when he began writing for the magazine, the *Herald of the Golden Age*. The journal was an early voice for vegetarianism, metaphysics, social reform, and practical spirituality.

His writing for the *Herald of the Golden Age* commenced a period of intensive creative activity. By 1901, his ideas bursting from years of study, he published his first book of spiritual philosophy, *From Poverty to Power*. The work extolled the creative agencies of thought, placing an equal emphasis on Christian-based ethics and New Thought motivation. In 1902, Allen launched his own spiritual magazine, the *Light of Reason,* later renamed *The Epoch.*

With 1903 came Allen's classic *As a Man Thinketh.* Although he considered the short work something of a minor effort, Lily admired it as an encapsulation of her husband's philosophy of self-help, ethical living, and mind-power metaphysics. Loosely based on Proverbs 23:7—"as a man thinketh in his heart, so is he"—the slender volume eventually became read around the world and brought Allen posthumous fame as one of the pioneering figures of modern inspirational thought.

There is no question in my mind that Allen is writing about himself in this passage from *As a Man Thinketh:*

> Here is a youth hard pressed by poverty and labor; confined long hours in an unhealthy workshop; unschooled, and lacking all the arts of refinement. But he dreams of better things: he thinks of intelligence, of refinement, of grace and beauty. He conceives of, mentally builds up, an ideal condition of life; vision of a wider liberty and a larger scope takes possession of him; unrest urges him to action, and he utilizes all his spare time and means, small though they are, to the development of his latent powers and resources. Very soon so altered has his mind become that the workshop can no longer hold him.

As with many of Allen's works, *As a Man Thinketh* was launched quietly, and its full impact was not felt until years after his death. Nonetheless, it won the fledgling author sufficient readership so that he was soon able to quit secretarial work and dedicate himself fully to writing and editing.

In the early 1900s, the family moved to the southern English coastal town of Ilfracombe, where he spent the rest of his life. He produced books at a remarkable pace—often more than one a year. With

Lily as his collaborator, Allen hosted discussion groups on metaphysical themes, continued publishing *The Epoch,* and spent long periods in nature, taking early morning walks and exploring the coastal highlands. He adopted a meticulous routine of meditating, writing, gardening, and walking. His work habits never flagged. "Thoroughness is genius," he wrote. Friends sensed that he was living out the simple, ascetic ideal of one of his heroes, Leo Tolstoy.

For all the vigor of his output, Allen suffered fragile health. Lily wrote of her husband growing ill in late 1911. On January 24, 1912, Allen died at home in Ilfracombe at age forty-seven, probably of tuberculosis. His body was cremated.

Lily continued to publish his remaining manuscripts, to work on her own books, and to edit and publish *The Epoch.* She also founded a New Thought–oriented society, the Union of Right Thinking. She died in 1952. Nora, a Spiritualist and later a devout Roman Catholic, died in 1976.

The legacy of James Allen is that the British contemplative established a practical philosophy of personal achievement set within an ethical and religious framework. Allen believed in precise, simple values of thrift, reliability, hard work, keeping one's word, respect of one's neighbor and employer, and a deeply held belief in the individual's power to radically alter his circumstances through proper exercise of thought.

In 1913, Lily Allen summarized her husband's mission in a preface to one of his posthumously published manuscripts, *Foundation Stones to Happiness and Success:* "He never wrote *theories,* or for the sake of writing; but he wrote when he had a message, and it became a message *only when he had lived it out in his own life,* and knew that it was good. Thus he wrote *facts,* which he had proven by practice."

AN EXPERIMENT IN GREATNESS

James Allen, and all of the figures we've been exploring, shared one trait: dedication to one overarching principle or ideal. In Allen's case, it was the transformative power of thought. Fealty to an ideal is the precondition to living with distinction. Revelation 3:16 rejects those who are undecided and without commitment: "So then because thou art lukewarm, and neither cold nor hot, I will spit thee out of my mouth." The hesitators, the vacillators, those who attempt no path—they receive nothing. Life permits no halfway measures.

Consider how rare it is that any of us today really strive to organize our lives around a deeply felt ethic. Most of the time we merely seek ways to win praise and security, particularly from peer groups that we want to enter or remain in. We go along, looking for whatever we believe we can realistically expect in money, prestige, and approval.

Taking inspiration from James Allen, I challenge you to an experiment that breaks with that approach to life. Are you willing to dedicate nine months, the gestation period of a new life, to relinquishing your conventional sense of security and redirecting your existence to a new, and possibly higher, principle—one of your own choosing?

First, I want you to select a book that expresses an ethical or spiritual outlook with which you passionately agree. Choose a work that has attained posterity, even if within a small circle, which confirms its pull on the moral imagination.

Your choice may be a sacred or ethical work such as the Tao Te Ching, Bhagavad Gita, Upanishads, Ethics of the Fathers, Meditations of Marcus Aurelius, or the Beatitudes. It may be a modern self-help book such as *Alcoholics Anonymous,* Napoleon Hill's *Think and Grow Rich,* or Viktor Frankl's *Man's Search for Meaning.* Or it may be an artist's or philosopher's vision of the good life such as Thoreau's *Walden,* Emerson's *Self-Reliance,* or any of James Allen's books, including those named in this chapter.

The core requirement is that your selection must summon you to a deeply felt, intimate goal or sense of purpose. The only restriction is that your chosen work must not require you to denigrate or obstruct another person's search or striving for his own highest potential.

At the back of your choice should be the perennial questions: What do I want? How do I want to live?

Then, dedicate yourself to your book and its ideas with unreserved passion for nine months.

I recommend not discussing what you're doing with anyone, with exceptions for members of a trusted support group, such as a prayer circle, twelve-step fellowship, or Master Mind alliance, a mutual support group based on the ideas of Napoleon Hill.* This is so you feel no pressure to submit your choices to the judgment of others, who may not share your values.

The spiritual teacher Krishnamurti taught that the biggest barrier to creativity and personal excellence is seeking out and clinging to "respectability." This is one of the maladies of modern life. A pioneer in the human potential movement once told me that positive thinking is "the simple man's philosophy." To me, that is not a negative description, or something to flee from. Contemporary people are overanxious to appear sophisticated and "beyond" certain ideas. The simple man's philosophy of positive thought animated James Allen's life—one of quiet, deliberative power.

Another trait that diverts our energies is conformity. We nest within our own subcultures and their attendant social and news media. We repeat what we're supposed to want, or what we claim to value, often (and sometimes subtly) parroting what we think makes us look good to others. We stand for nothing. Hence, we never realize what we're capable of.

Are you willing to risk all that for nine months?

In committing to an ethical idea, you must also be willing for your idea to be wrong. If your selected idea proves faulty or false, or if its pursuit fills you with sorrow and frustration rather than a feeling of vivifying clarity (or moments of such), that may provide a course correction in your search for truth. And if it proves right, if it builds your

---

*I explore this in my book *The Power of the Master Mind.*

sense of expectancy and calm, you are then delivered to a higher state of conduct from which to push on with your search.

You may also find yourself drifting away from the book you first selected. You may experience events that make its ideas seem less compelling, or you may notice yourself experiencing indifference, conflict, or forgetfulness toward your previously embraced ideal (the last of these is the most common). If you can steer yourself back to your book, then do so—but don't fight the urge to reconsider your selection.

For example, in my personal embarkation on this experiment, I selected Neville Goddard's book of lectures *Immortal Man,* a compelling record of his philosophy of the divinity of imagination. Whether I follow Neville's ideas with totality is beside the point (I address this later); the real adventure and sense of self-discovery was in applying and testing one ethical goal in my life, namely: Is the mind the builder of all circumstance? Despite my enthusiastic beginning, my attention drifted. Other ideas and possibilities interposed themselves. I gravitated toward Nietzsche's *Beyond Good and Evil,* as translated by Walter Kaufmann. In that book, I found a set of ideas that seemed to confirm, focus, and sharpen an instinct at which I had previously and independently arrived, but which Nietzsche captured with unparalleled precision and authority: "A living thing seeks above all to *discharge* its strength—life itself is *will to power;* self-preservation is only one of the indirect and most frequent *results.*"

Nietzsche's concerns in *Beyond Good and Evil* are the need to see through to the primary nature of things; to avoid the confusion of forms, artifice, and consensual principles and premises—all of which disrupt or destroy the human search. The quality of seeing through to the thing itself, of attempting to discern and act in compact with authentic nature, have much in common with ideals expressed by Emerson. Nietzsche's thought, while immensely readable, does not have the exquisite simplicity of Neville's and does not necessarily comport with—or contradict—Neville's philosophy of the divinity of imagination. In any case, Nietzsche's ideas called to me, possibly converging with Neville's theology of self-primacy. *Beyond Good and Evil* became the guiding light of my experiment. It remains so as I write these words.

Think how wonderful it could be to invest yourself fully in one ideal. Again, the point is not to be settled or *right* on the matter; the point is to test life's boundaries against the weight of a principle.

The very act of living for something immediately gives you an improved sense of self-possession and purpose. You experience the sensation of being "consciously right, superior, and happy," as William James wrote in *The Varieties of Religious Experience*. You are set apart.

I challenge you: Select one sacred or ethical book. Live by its principles for nine months. Dedicate yourself to its ideal with total commitment and unreserved abandon. Attempt, for a time, to live a principle-based life, as James Allen did. See what happens.

CHAPTER EIGHT

THE ETHIC
OF GETTING RICH

There is a conflict in early twenty-first century New Thought. Some seekers want a New Thought that emphasizes personal attainment and ambition. Others believe that New Thought's focus should be on social justice—they view the think-and-grow-rich approach as narrow, unspiritual, or outdated.

The 1910 classic *The Science of Getting Rich* by mind-power pioneer and social activist Wallace D. Wattles (1860–1911) points the way out of this conflict. Wattles's message is distinctly relevant for a contemporary New Thought culture that is divided between social justice and personal achievement. The author and Progressive Era reformer demonstrated how these two priorities are really one.

A socialist, a Quaker, and an early theorist of mind-positive metaphysics, Wattles taught that the true aim of enrichment is not accumulation of personal resources alone, but also the establishment of a more equitable world, one of shared abundance and possibility. He believed that combining mind-power mechanics with an ardent dedication to self-improvement—while rejecting a narrowly competitive, *me-first* ethos—makes you part of an interlinking chain that leads to a more prosperous dynamic for everyone.

Wattles's slender guidebook *The Science of Getting Rich* remained obscure in mainstream culture until about 2007. Around that time, *The Science of Getting Rich* became known as a key source behind Rhonda Byrne's *The Secret*. The century-old book began hitting bestseller lists. I published a paperback edition myself that hit number one on the *Bloomberg Businessweek* list. My 2016 audio condensation reached number two on iTunes.

What many of Wattles's twenty-first-century readers miss, however, is his dedication to the ethic of cooperative advancement above competition and his belief that competition itself is an outmoded idea, due to be supplanted once humanity discovers the ever-renewing creative capacities of the mind. As none but the most perceptive readers could detect, Wattles combined his mind metaphysics with a dollop of Marxist language. His outlook was idealistic—perhaps extravagant—but he attempted to live up to it.

A onetime Methodist minister, Wattles lost his northern Indiana pulpit when he refused collection-basket offerings from congregants who owned sweatshops. He twice ran for office on the ticket of fellow Hoosier Eugene V. Debs's Socialist Party, first for Congress and again as a close second for mayor of Elwood, Indiana. At the time of his death in 1911, he and his daughter, Florence (1888–1947)—a powerful socialist orator in her own right and later the publicity director at publisher E. P. Dutton—were laying the groundwork for a new mayoral run, cut short when he died of tuberculosis at age fifty while traveling to Tennessee.

Florence wrote to Eugene Debs's brother, Theodore, on January 30, 1935. Addressing him as "Dear Comrade," she lovingly recalled her father as "a remarkable personality, and a beautiful spirit, which, to me, at least, has never died."*

Was Wattles's vision of New Thought metaphysics and social reform really so utopian? We live in an age at which he would have

---

*Archived in Indiana State University's Wabash Valley Visions & Voices Digital Memory Project.

marveled—yet also recognized: physicians perform successful placebo surgeries, and demonstrate the placebo response in weight loss, eyesight, and even in instances where placebos are transparently administered; in the field called neuroplasticity, brain scans reveal that neural pathways are "rewired" by thought patterns—a biologic fact of mind over matter; quantum physics experiments, as will later be seen, pose extraordinary questions about the intersection between thought and object; and serious ESP experiments repeatedly demonstrate the nonphysical conveyance of information in laboratory settings. Wattles's mission, now more than a century old, was to ask whether these abilities, only hinted at in the science of his day, could be personally applied and tested on the material and social scales of life.

He did not live to see the influence of his book. But his calm certainty and confident yet gentle tone suggest that he felt assured of his ideas. Like every sound thinker, Wattles left us not with a doctrine, but with articles of experimentation. The finest thing you can do to honor the memory of this good man—and to advance on your own path in life—is to heed his advice: Go and experiment with the capacities of your mind. Go and try. And if you experience results, do as he did: tell the people.

A NEW VISION OF MIND POWER

We are at a propitious moment to reexamine Wattles. The New Thought movement, as noted, is conflicted between urges to "change the world" or "be on top of the world." This tension may be the chrysalis from which a new approach emerges.

Here is a starting point: In her 2016 blog article *Why the Self-Help Industry Isn't Changing the World,* spiritual counselor and writer Andréa Ranae raised excellent points about why today's self-help culture deals poorly with social questions. Like Ranae, I have had the experience of witnessing a tragedy in the world only to log onto social media to find the usual population of motivational gurus prattling away like nothing has happened, offering the standard you-can-do-it nostrums. Or, in awkwardly acknowledging a tragic event, they might show an image like a cake with a candle blown out, or some similarly cloying gesture. Like Ranae, I've never believed that the New Thought and self-help movements should stand aloof from human events.*

But Ranae argues a deeper point, which is that many of the problems people bring to her as a spiritual counselor are actually symptoms of an unjust world; it feels to her like she's avoiding the point if she treats the personal symptom and not the larger cause.

I honor that point—but I approach these matters somewhat differently. Human nature, in its complexities, is twisted into knots, some of them resulting from outer circumstances, and some from within ourselves. That will always be the case. I do not want to see an overly politicized New Thought in the twenty-first century. I do not want a New Thought that is closed off to people who are, in fact, suspicious of "social action," which can quickly devolve into posturing, vague pronouncements, and inertia. People harbor vastly—and justly— different ideas of social polity. Indeed, a poorly defined social-justice model in New Thought can actually deemphasize the pursuit of individual attainment, which is historically vital to New Thought's appeal. I must also add that, in my experience, some of the loudest proponents of social justice in our spiritual communities cannot be counted on to water a houseplant. If you want social justice, I often tell people, begin with the ethic of keeping your word and excelling at the basics of organization and planning. Start there—and if you perform well at those things, expand your vision. You cannot "fix" things that affect others unless you can first care for the things that are your own.

In my 2014 book *One Simple Idea,* I wrote critically of success guru Napoleon Hill. I saw the *Think and Grow Rich* author as someone who moved the dial away from social justice in the American metaphysical tradition. But, in retrospect, I was wrong. It's not that my criticism of

---

*E.g., see my "What Does New Thought Say about War?" post at HarvBishop.com.

Hill was off target; the writer made pronouncements and did things to which I object. But Hill's greatness as a metaphysician and motivational thinker was to frame a truly workable program of ethical, *individual* success. He owed no apology for that. One online writer recently wrote a bellicose, drawn-out article impugning Hill's character. But the one historically significant thing about Hill is *his work,* and you cannot evaluate the man absent that—any more than the sensationalistic biographer Albert Goldman could capture the characters of John Lennon or Elvis Presley, two of his subjects, without understanding them as artists. Hill's success program has earned its posterity, which I know from personal experience.

New Thought at its best and most infectious celebrates the primacy of the individual. Seen in a certain light, the mystical teacher Neville Goddard, the New Thought figure whom I most admire, was a kind of *spiritualized objectivist.* Or perhaps I could say that Ayn Rand, the founder of philosophical Objectivism, and an ardent atheist, was a secularized Neville. Neville and Rand each espoused a form of extremist self-responsibility. Objective reality, each taught, is a fact of life. The motivated person must *select* among the possibilities and circumstances of reality. In their view, the individual is solely responsible, ultimately, for what he does with his choices. Rand saw this selection as the exercise of personal will and rational judgment; Neville saw it as vested in the creative instrumentalities of your imagination. But both espoused the same principle: the world that you occupy is your own obligation.

Is there a dichotomy between Neville's radical individualism and the communal vision of Wattles? Not for me. As noted earlier, I'm skeptical toward language such as inner/outer, essence/ego, spiritual/material, which buzzes around many of our alternative spiritual communities. Not only do opposites attract, but paradoxes complete. It is in the nature of life. There are no neat lines of division in the territory of truth. Neville's vision of individual excellence, and Wattles's ideal of community enrichment are inextricably bound because New

Thought—unlike secular Objectivism and varying forms of ceremonial magick or Thelemic philosophy—functions along the lines of Scriptural ethics. New Thought does not countenance an exclusivist society. It promulgates a radically karmic ethos, in which the thoughts and actions enacted toward others simultaneously play out toward the self; doing unto others *is* doing unto self—the part and the whole are inseparable.

Those of us involved with New Thought are, in fact, always striving to see life as "one thing." That one thing—call it the Creative Power or Higher Mind in which we all function—can expand in infinite directions. Must a seeker choose between a nice car and "awareness"? Must I choose between Wallace D. Wattles and Neville? Both were bold, beautiful, and right in many ways; both had a vision of ultimate freedom—of the creative individual determining rather than bending to circumstance.

Rather than propose a political program for New Thought, I instead want to strike at the blithe, sometimes childish tone that pervades much of its culture. Within churches, meetings, and discussion groups, people who think seriously about current events or ethical problems are sometimes regarded as missing the proper spirit. Yet thoughtful adults are not supposed to be Mr. Roarke saying, "Smiles everyone, smiles!" (Young people, work with me . . .) Indeed, some New Thoughters even express boredom with discussions of world issues or are grievously uninformed about such things. I was once making a point to a New Thought minister, and he gestured with his hand from the base of his neck to the top of his skull and said, "That sounds very *here up*." I was being too intellectual, he felt. Such prohibitions do not foster a well-rounded movement.

Rather than venture political agendas, we must improve the intellectual tenor of New Thought—and avoid leaning on catechism when topics of tragedy or injustice arise. A familiar New Thought refrain is that someone who has experienced tragedy, either on a personal or mass scale, was somehow thinking in comportment with the grievous event. That is indefensible. We are, in fact, always thinking about different needs and possibilities, shifting among competing thoughts and interests; the key factor in whether a thought becomes determinative, as seen in psychical and placebo studies as well as in the testimony of individual seekers, is when emotional force and sublime focus combine in a single thought. How can a swath of people, whether in a country or as pedestrians at an event, be classified as forming a discernable mental whole? I'm not saying that there isn't mass psychology. Following traumatic events, and during moments of heightened crowd stimulation (such as hearing a powerful speech), a kind of herd psychology or groupthink can certainly take hold. But preceding such events, human thoughts are frenetic and unruly, often as busied and individualized as movements on a crowded street. I see no evidence of a group will to suffer.

Just as there is no sole cause, nor a single mental law, behind tragedies, there is no one answer when analyzing politics or current events. But what no serious spiritual movement can sustain is having *no answer* or *no response*. Or no discussion. Or no perspective. I would rather enter a roomful of people who civilly disagree on problematic issues than are blissfully indifferent, or who run from discussion as though from contagion, which is the default to which some New Thoughters have wed themselves.

This kind of studied indifference is the problem that Andréa Ranae is putting her finger on. It is a serious one. Yet historically it was *not* a problem for pioneers like Wallace Wattles or his publisher, Elizabeth Towne, a leading New Thought voice and suffragist activist. In 1926, Towne was elected the first female alderman in Holyoke, Massachusetts. Two years later she mounted an unsuccessful independent bid for mayor. Progressive Era pioneers of New Thought like Towne, Wattles, Helen Wilmans, Ralph Waldo Trine, and many of their contemporaries, were socially and intellectually well rounded. They took seriously both the spiritual and public dimensions of life. Their expansive outlooks were a natural expression of their driving curiosity and engagement with the world. If we can foster a better, fuller intellectual culture within New Thought (which is one of the aims of this book), I think the poles of social action and personal betterment would naturally converge.

A coalescing of interests does not mean that New Thoughters will agree on social issues, or vote the same. It means that New Thought values and methods will shine the way for each seeker, whatever his values or circumstances, to shape his life—and the world—in accordance with his highest self.

CHAPTER NINE

WHY THE CRITICS
ARE WRONG

If you've read this far in this book, you probably take seriously the question of thought and causality. And I am fairly confident that if you've read this far, you've probably noticed, like me, a lot of criticism of self-help, positive thinking, and New Thought methods in the media over the last ten or so years, typified by headlines like "The 'Tyranny' of Positive Thinking (*Newsweek,* 2016); "A Harvard Psychologist Explains Why Forcing Positive Thinking Won't Make You Happy" (*Washington Post,* 2016); and "The Problem with Positive Thinking" (*New York Times* op-ed, 2014).* You may have heard friends, family members, or social-media interlocutors making fun of "woo-woo" from time to time. In this chapter, I want to supply you with information that affirms your deepest instincts that our minds are tools of influence—and that cynics are wrong about positive thinking.

Criticism of self-help, mental therapeutics, and positive-mind philosophy has become so common in our journalistic and academic culture that editors and critics themselves do not even recognize it as such. Several months before writing these words, I approached an

---

*For more on this trend, see my articles at Medium.com, "Losing the War on Unhappiness" (9/19/16) and "The War on Positive Thinking" (9/23/16).

opinion editor at a major newspaper, someone with whom I'd worked previously, to pitch an opinion piece that defended positive-mind philosophy from its critics and pushed back against the intellectual vogue in trashing positive thinking. He rejected the idea, explaining that he felt I was arguing with a straw man. Weeks later, the same opinion page reran—*reran*—a piece from two years earlier that impugned the popularity of positive thinking. I wrote back suggesting that since an intellectual battle *did* seem to be afoot, and using the rerun piece (among others) as an exhibit, why not consider a debate feature in which several writers contend over the question? Well, he replied, then it just seems like we're retreading an old argument. . . . It was a Catch-22.

Many of the same journalists, social critics, and intellectuals who run down positive thinking, New Age, and self-help are all too eager to cite cognitive studies as proof of a favored idea because such reports seem to possess the sheen of peer-reviewed, clinically based sturdiness. A case in point arrived in 2015 with an article in the online opinion journal *Aeon,* in which journalist and social critic Elizabeth Svoboda sized up the self-help field. In her "Saved by the Book," Svoboda concluded that some cognitively based self-help books are effective—and well worth defending—while New Age and positive-thinking books are the product of "woo-peddlers" who cheapen the field.

Svoboda's piece demonstrated two assumptions that make it difficult to gainfully discuss self-help therapeutics in much of today's media. First, the author groups together two different kinds of books: metaphysical works, such as the perennial critics's punching bag *The Secret,* and books based on clinical study, such as *Feeling Good* by David D. Burns, M.D. Although their authors share some concerns, such books have little in common: one represents theology and the other cognitive therapy.

Around the same time, this dissonance manifested in the pages of *Publishers Weekly,* the publishing trade journal, when an anonymous reviewer (isn't it time we have done with anonymous reviews?) lamented the absence of material on "cognitive restructuring" in Richard Smoley's 2015 slender masterpiece *The Deal,* a spiritual program of forgiveness, which I published at TarcherPerigee. It goes without saying that a critic is free to dislike something; I personally venerate the book and believe that it's one of the most worthwhile things I've published. But to criticize a spiritual philosopher for not supplying cognitive data is simply to change the writer's subject.

The second, and more serious, assumption in Svoboda's critique comes in her uncritical acceptance of clinical studies that are "calling out the woo-peddlers." This generally means experiments that purport to show how positive thinking is ineffective and even counterproductive. Having read some of those studies, more on which shortly, I've found that what they often show is that "fringe thinking" doesn't work: that is, uncritical optimism and uncritical pessimism, to the exclusion of constructive action or subtlety.

With regard to empiricism, Svoboda does not mention recent studies that deepen our questions about the affirmative powers of the mind, such as the aforementioned "honest placebo" study at Harvard, where subjects reported relief even when knowingly receiving a fake pill, or Harvard psychologist Ellen Langer's studies of aging in which elderly people experienced reversals of psychological and physical decline when immersed in nostalgic settings designed to evoke feelings of youth.

Mainstream media frequently plays punch the smiley face. On February 13, 2014, the *New Yorker* ran a critique of positive thinking in which researchers concluded that affirmative-mind mechanics make you lazy or inert. The piece began (spoiler alert) with a swipe at *The Secret* and went on to quote Heather Barry Kappes, a management professor at the London School of Economics: "Imagining a positive outcome conveys the sense that you're approaching your goals, which takes the edge off the need to achieve."

I wonder how many people who have immersed themselves in positive-mind metaphysics—as opposed to the students who participated in Kappes's two-week study*—would recognize their experience in her statement? I don't see my personal experience in it. I didn't publish my first books until I was well into my forties—and the result grew from years of labor, visualization, prayer, focus, and affirmation. As with health, I encourage a D-day approach: Throw everything you've got at your objective. If this two-week experiment had continued for say, two years, maybe Kappes's undergraduate subjects would have learned things about themselves. Perhaps they would have discovered that a mixture of self-affirmation, action, and meditation is helpful. But who can derive corrective lessons from a week of visualization and another of viewing the results? Even a subjective study of redirecting your thoughts and recording results, which I proposed in the November 2015 issue of *Science of Mind* magazine, lasted thirty days.

In fairness, researchers have also subjected positive thinking to long-term studies, including a two-year experiment in career visualization with German university students.† The researchers discovered that students who imagined positive outcomes to their job search were more likely to experience disappointing results; but the subjects who harbored "positive expectations" were more likely to succeed. And this is where the study's terms and methods get curious: "Though the role of positive expectations of success in finding work is amply demonstrated," the researchers wrote in their rationale for the study, "the role of fantasy has been neglected." So, their focus was not positive thinking, per se, but imaginal fantasy. How many detractors of positive thinking, such as social critic Barbara Ehrenreich—whose work will be considered shortly—would pause over (or even notice) that sentence and consider whether they had carved out distinctions in their own writing between

---

*"Positive Fantasies about Idealized Futures Sap Energy" by Heather Barry Kappes and Gabriele Oettingen, *Journal of Experimental Social Psychology* 47 (2011). See "Study 3: Fantasies and Actual Accomplishment."
†"The Motivating Function of Thinking about the Future: Expectations Versus Fantasies" by Gabriele Oettingen and Doris Mayer, *Journal of Personality and Social Psychology* 83, no. 5 (2002).

"positive expectations" and "fantasy" (by which the researchers seemed to mean visualization)? And what would such a distinction look like? Our psychology is a mosaic of images, scenes, emotions, and words.

The researchers concluded: "students with high expectations of success received comparatively more job offers and earned more money; students experiencing positive fantasies, to the contrary, received comparatively fewer job offers and earned less money." Here is an example of how "fringe thinking" can get conflated with "positive thinking": The researchers did not discover that positive thinkers earned less; rather, they found that positive fantasizers seemed to perform less well, while negative fantasizers were not studied.

One consideration that apparently concerned neither the study's authors nor the journalists covering them (the study was also part of the *New Yorker* critique and widely picked up from there) was whether any of these researchers were capable of guiding their subjects in meaningful methods of positive-mind dynamics. Their techniques are not described. Did they approximate the virtuosity and inventiveness of, say, a mental-conditioning pioneer such as Émile Coué? What, in the end, was really tested? (Perhaps it was the researchers' abilities as motivational coaches.)

Regardless of the gaps, these kinds of studies translate into snappy news coverage, as reflected in the *New Yorker*'s headline: "The Powerlessness of Positive Thinking." But such experiments rarely receive scrutiny from writers and researchers who are actually immersed in the practice and consideration of positive-mind metaphysics. Unfortunately, such people number near zero in academia. (This situation also gives me concern—why isn't the New Thought culture more intellectually dynamic? Christian Science has produced formidable scholars from within its ranks, such as Robert Peel and Stephen Gottschalk. So has Mormonism. New Thought has lagged in this regard.)

Because the intellectual culture denigrates terms like New Age and positive thinking, even positive-psychology pioneer Martin Seligman has rushed to disavow any connection to the "power of positive thinking," which he describes as passive and unscientifically wishful. As I've written in *One Simple Idea,* some of the finest voices in New Thought and positive-mind metaphysics in the early twentieth century, including French hypnotherapist Coué and American minister John Herman Randall, prescribed methods that square with current protocols in neuroplasticity and cognitive psychology. There is no simple way of dismissing or proscribing positive thinking. In fact, a better line of distinction for Seligman would be that New Thought has historically been spiritual in nature—it employs a metaphysical outlook that posits our thoughts as a channel of higher creative power or extraphysicality, versus Seligman's focus on devising sounder psychological patterns. For this reason, I, too, see differences between New Thought and positive psychology, but for reasons other than Seligman's.

All of this leaves us with a situation where positivity-based psychologists like Seligman are eager to distance themselves from their own intellectual forebears, and most journalists lack the forum (or instinct) to discuss whether spiritual self-help books may, in fact, dramatically improve lives—and do so more fully, in some cases, than books that aspire to clinical validation.

The endurance of New Thought–oriented classics, ranging from *As a Man Thinketh* (1903) to *Psycho-Cybernetics* (1960), rests on the broad and even epic nature of their philosophy. Such works impart meaning and provide an ethical path to follow, with the aim of developing the whole person. Most clinicians and researchers, however, disregard, if not denigrate, individual testimony from New Agers, positive thinkers, and twelve-step group members.

And this, finally, exposes the core challenge of evaluating books of spiritual self-help: Researchers are not trained or inclined to consider personal testimony. This problem extends back to the days of William James, who noted that many Victorian-era scientists (like many cognitive researchers today) regarded personal testimony as fickle, obfuscating, and scientifically useless, rather than one part of a valid record. Svoboda quotes psychologist Joanne V. Wood of the University of Waterloo, a current critic of spiritual self-help, dismissing the experiences of New Age readers: "Concluding that it works based on personal experience does not constitute rigorous research." Fair enough. But if a certain type of testimony coalesces into a comparative record across decades, is that not to be considered?

Historically, researchers have found it difficult to study Alcoholics Anonymous—a fluid, nonsectarian fellowship where people come and go. This is all the more reason to regard the testimony of AA members as an important link in understanding the endurance of the twelve-step approach. And, given some of the concerns I've raised above, I think it's questionable that the past decade's critical experiments in positive-mind therapeutics would prove any more definitive or repeatable than the experiences of participants in metaphysical thought systems such as AA, Science of Mind, and Unity.

It is natural for people to "shop around" for religions or spiritual movements that fit their needs. I have friends and family members who have benefited immeasurably from twelve-step programs, mindfulness meditation, or new religious movements such as Mormonism and Christian Science—and I know others for whom such approaches are anathema. I have found great help in my own life from mystical philosophers such as Neville Goddard and Vernon Howard, and the practice of Transcendental Meditation. None of this proves that one system or another works. Rather, it demonstrates, as does a vast record of personal testimony, that the experience of the individual—the very thing that Professor Wood dismisses—is a vital element in understanding spiritual self-help.

My personal observation is that the classics of self-help—such as *Alcoholics Anonymous* (1939) and *Think and Grow Rich* (1937)—retain a unique hold across generations and benefit from considerable word-of-mouth recommendation, which suggests something far more than faddish appeal or a revolving door of gullible readers. It has been my sense that the effectiveness of such books rests heavily on the passion of the individual seeker. As an Arab proverb goes: "The way bread tastes depends on how hungry you are." Your depth of hunger for self-change is likely to match the benefit you experience from any legitimate self-help program.

I applaud Svoboda for opening this discussion and arguing for those works of practical psychology that she has found personally meaningful. But we are a long way from finding proper ground in mainstream media and scholarship to seriously consider—without apology or embarrassment—the efficacy of the "woo-peddlers."

While Svoboda honestly considers the case for and against self-help, a less principled and more widespread critique has recently emerged from the work of Barbara Ehrenreich. The social critic's 2009 bestseller *Bright-Sided* was a scathing and influential indictment of positive thinking, which set the tone for much of the criticism of positive thinking found in the work we've reviewed, and generally throughout the intellectual culture.

Let me be clear about my allegiances: One of the most influential books I read in college was Ehrenreich's brilliant critique of gender politics, *The Hearts of Men*. As I neared my senior year I became an active member of the Democratic Socialists of America, the organization that Ehrenreich co-chaired along with my hero, author and activist Michael Harrington. I remain a member thirty years later.

I've attended political conferences with Ehrenreich, including one slightly zany retreat at a private zoo and estate in North Florida where, in between discussions of how to revive the American left, we toured open-air refuges for African wildlife (and I hoped that we hadn't stepped into a remake of *The Most Dangerous Game*).

Like many of Ehrenreich's admirers, I had always found her trenchant, formidable, sometimes frustrating, and unfailingly insightful. That changed when she adopted her current role as the literary nemesis of the positive-thinking movement. The notion that thoughts are causative takes many different forms, of course, varyingly expressed in metaphysical or psychological terms, or both. Ehrenreich groups together this whole thought movement as proffering a myopic batch of illusions, which serve to reinforce existing power structures. She explored this thesis in *Bright-Sided* and in many interviews and appearances that followed. Ehrenreich revisited this perspective in a December 31, 2015, op-ed in the *New York Times,* where she critiqued what she saw as the vacuity of the current research into the benefits of gratitude. She quickly connected the "current hoopla around gratitude" with her real target: positive thinking, which she sees typified in the excesses of *The Secret* and the foolhardy exuberance that she blames for the Great Recession of 2008. (Goldman Sachs, take a breather—Norman Vincent Peale, brace yourself.)

Rarely has the *Times* published such an articulate (and damning) selection of reader objections to an opinion piece. My own didn't make the cut, so I'll provide it here:

> *To the Editor,*
>
> *Polemics for or against gratitude, or certain kinds of gratitude, edge us toward angels-on-pinheads arguments. In essence, Barbara Ehrenreich pits her conception of gratefulness against someone else's, whether in the form of platitudes, questionable studies, or the every-ready critical punching bag* The Secret *(which turns ten this year, by the way—maybe it's time to give it a rest). There is, in fact, no innate tension between gratitude in the social sense, which Ms. Ehrenreich calls for, and gratitude in the spiritual sense, which she finds iffy. Given that most of us in the West are, by global standards, the wealthiest, healthiest, and safest people on earth, gratitude should be considered simply a form of realism.*
>
> *Sincerely,*
> *Mitch Horowitz*
> *January 1, 2016*

The *Times* has graciously used several of my letters responding to polemics against positive thinking. But I believe that they made the right judgment in bypassing this one in order to make room for other correspondents, including a UC Berkeley researcher Jason Marsh who said that Ehrenreich misstated his and his colleagues' research on gratitude by omitting the researchers' key point that authentic gratitude must be accompanied by empathy and a feeling of a strengthened social ties, a topic he explored in an online essay of his own, "What Barbara Ehrenreich Gets Wrong about Gratitude."

That important critique falls second, in my mind, to a heartfelt statement the *Times* used from the very type of working person for whom Ehrenreich strives to speak—but barely seems to recognize:

To the Editor,

I was so disheartened by Barbara Ehrenreich's leap to assume that it's selfish to find personal empowerment through positive thinking and gratitude. It's ironic for me personally that she points to the crash of 2008 as an excellent reason for people to have abandoned "silly" positive thinking.

When my husband and I almost lost our house that year, struggling with health insurance premiums and a new baby, I discovered the exact self-help messages that she's dismissing, and they kept me afloat mentally so that I could focus on a plan to get work, and get us out of our hole. I was in despair, and found that making lists of things I could be thankful for brought me some happiness, then more happiness—and, yes, it did feel good, thank you very much!

And I wasn't selfish. I dug myself out of an onslaught of depression, and when we got back on track financially, I did practice a "vigorous and inclusive" gratitude by giving back to people who needed it. There's another self-help cliché about putting your own oxygen mask on first, then helping others, and you simply can't do that without first practicing personal (selfish?) gratitude.

Paula Tiberius
North Hollywood, CA
January 9, 2016

Ehrenreich's critique of positive thinking in *Bright-Sided* rests on the notion that positive-mind therapeutics harmfully encourage people to see what they want to—rather than to deal with, challenge, and improve the world as it is. But when paddling into the waters of positive-mind philosophy, she imitates the same intellectual blindness that she aims to pillory. It is, frankly, difficult to tell whether this stems from laziness of research or a willful neglect of facts for the sake of scoring a witty point. In *Bright-Sided* not one note is made of the longtime radical and progressive history of the positive-thinking movement. As alluded to earlier, positive-mind philosophy was interwoven with the reformist ideals of the Progressive Era. Its early explorers and acolytes included feminist pioneer Elizabeth Cady Stanton, New Deal icon Henry Wallace, and black nationalist Marcus Garvey.* Of course, there are also examples to the contrary (and she finds them). But to omit the progressive aspect of positive thinking is akin to omitting the history of civil rights and labor organizing when writing the history of the Democratic party.

This historical shallowness is further seen in how she deals with the fundamental influence of Ralph Waldo Emerson on the popular American psyche and on the positive-thinking movement in particular: Almost all of her quotes from Emerson are referenced to secondary sources, primarily Catherine Albanese's 2007 scholarly (and magisterial) study of transcendental religions in America, *A Republic of Mind and Spirit*. If a freshman quoted Emerson from secondary sources in a term paper, I'd have questions for that student. But how can the leading critic of positive-mind mechanics evidently not have read and yellow-highlighted essays by the very philosopher who made the movement possible to begin with?

In her *Times* piece, Ehrenreich dusted off criticism of the mega-selling book and movie *The Secret*—a work now ten years old—to claim

---

*See "The Hidden History of New Thought" by Harvey Bishop, *Science of Mind*, September 2015. I also explore these themes in my books *Occult America* and *One Simple Idea*.

that its excesses have wholly exposed the "silliness" of positive thinking. I have criticized *The Secret* in blunt terms in *One Simple Idea* and elsewhere. But, more importantly than that popular work, we are, as noted, living through a period of new findings in placebo research, ranging from placebo surgeries to myriad studies linking positive expectancy to a strengthened immunological response, as well as widely accepted findings in the nascent field of neuroplasticity, in which redirected thoughts are seen to alter brain biology. These developments in mental therapeutics are deepening our questions about the potentialities of the mind. Given that such things are reported in media Ehrenreich presumably encounters, from the *New York Times Magazine* to NPR, as well as in medical journals, it is intellectually lame to fall back on berating *The Secret*.

She also blames positive thinking for the 2008 financial crash, a point of view popularized in a December 2009 cover story in *The Atlantic* by journalist Hanna Rosin. I disagree with Rosin's challenging conclusions that prosperity ministries inspired a boundless faith in our shaky economy and triggered the crash. I think Rosin gives too much credit to the influence of prosperity ministers and lays insufficient blame on coercive lending tactics. But, nonetheless, Rosin performed extraordinary reportorial legwork and research, exploring the lives of day-to-day people—a lot like the North Hollywood correspondent above—who staked part of their financial well-being, for good or ill, on the validity of positive thinking and affirmative prayer.

By contrast, Ehrenreich took the easy road: She visited megachurches, such as Joel Osteen's in Texas, and did her best to paint a depressing, Hopperesque canvas of lost American dreamers pinning their hopes on positivity ministers like Osteen, whose height and appearance she derided. What she omitted was any measured critique of what Osteen actually says.

After the 2008 crash, Osteen, speaking from his televised Sunday morning pulpit, addressed the question of what someone should do if he or she fears being laid off. He offered three pieces of advice: (1) constantly learn new technology and skills, (2) continually take on additional tasks at work, and (3) demonstrate a positive mental attitude at work. Ehrenreich would probably roll her eyes at this kind of page-a-day calendar advice, noting that it does nothing for any serious person—right? Wrong. This is exactly the kind of advice that I would give to any member of my own family, while at the same time working to restore the kinds of banking regulations, unionization, and transparency in lending that had protected us from this kind of disastrous crash following the Great Depression.

Ehrenreich seems to believe that practical advice and political reform are at odds. That is, simply, ridiculous. Practicality and protest go hand in hand. The revolution does not solve my problems next Thursday. For that, I need help that conforms to the boundaries we currently live in, while fighting to expand them. After all these years of the American left wandering in the wilderness, does this really require restating?

And, as one of the *Times* correspondents pointed out, some of the most effective social reformers in American history have been "happy warriors"—hopeful, dynamic people who related to ordinary Americans, or who were themselves ordinary Americans, and who would never dream of casually debasing popular religious or therapeutic ideas. This was true, for example, of Ehrenreich's Democratic Socialists of America co-chair Michael Harrington, who died of cancer in 1989. Mike, as he was known to all, felt great affection for people and evoked similar feelings in return. As one of my old comrades Dinah Leventhal recalled: "He really loved this country and thought that you had to love the country to be a radical, to be a socialist, and to want to change it." You cannot love a country in any authentic sense when you offhandedly disparage—and make no effort to take full measure of—an outlook embraced by varied millions of Americans, of all backgrounds and classes.

Mike's biographer Maurice Isserman noted, with trademark restraint, that Ehrenreich "did not get along with Michael." (It is the sole mention of her in Isserman's biography *The Other American*.) This was pretty common knowledge back in the day—and it may have revealed the seedlings of Ehrenreich's current jag against positive thinking. She is convinced—and tries to convince others—that the positive-mind tradition and expressions of American optimism represent an inherently selfish, capitalist-bolstering, mush-headed philosophy that serves to keep workers in their place. She may need to see it that way—such a view may affirm the oppositional tone and sense of outsider exclusivism that, in effect, tell her who she is.

Ehrenreich's readers, who trust her as a straight-shooting social critic, are being misled about the history and varied approaches of positive thinking. But these readers do not, and likely never will, realize that they are being misled. This is because self-help and positive-thinking literature is perhaps the one form of writing whose detractors feel no obligation to read or test-drive before promulgating an opinion. Recall the journalist in chapter 1 who traveled around the world to visit the Maharishi but never attempted Transcendental Meditation. There is a word for this type of thinking: cynicism. It is the same type of predetermined thought that Ehrenreich perceives in positive thinking.

There is an important critical discussion to be had about the problems (and possibilities) of this hugely popular American philosophy. Ehrenreich could have begun that discussion with the note on which she opened her book, recalling the nightmarish conformity of being encouraged to think positively following a cancer diagnosis. I have recounted similarly appalling episodes. But Ehrenreich seems to have decided aforethought not to leave the door open—not even by a crack—for the possibility that there is more to this philosophy than a smiley face holding a mallet. That is a disservice to the career of a valuable social critic and the readers who believe in her.

The year that Indiana socialist and New Thought pioneer Wallace D. Wattles died, 1911, also saw the publication of his final book, *The Science of Being Great*. In it, Wattles paid tribute to American socialist icon Eugene V. Debs (you'll recall that daughter Florence Wattles corresponded with Debs's brother). Debs was, before Norman Thomas and Bernie Sanders, the most famous socialist ever to run for president. Wattles wrote of him:

> Mr. Debs reverences humanity. No appeal for help is ever made to him in vain. No one receives from him an unkind or censorious word. You cannot come into his presence without being made sensible of his deep and kindly personal interest in you. Every person, be he millionaire, grimy workingman, or toil worn woman, receives the radiant warmth of a brotherly affection that is sincere and true. No ragged child speaks to him on the street without receiving instant and tender recognition. Debs loves men. This has made him the leading figure in a great movement, the beloved hero of a million hearts, and will give him a deathless name.

If the fortunes of the American left, as a cohesive and ongoing movement in our national life, are to be sustained, this kind of ideal requires emulation. The failure of much of the mainstream intelligentsia to understand what the interior of the nation was thinking about in the 2016 presidential election can been seen, in capsule form, in its dismissal of positive-thinking philosophy, as championed by Ehrenreich. Positive thinking is not the enemy of progress—nor is it the sole solution to retrograde problems. Rather, positive-mind philosophy, which remains hugely popular, is a misunderstood and deeply felt aspect of the American psyche, which no one who hopes to reach the heart of our nation can afford to disparage or ignore.

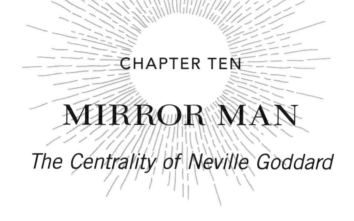

CHAPTER TEN

MIRROR MAN

The Centrality of Neville Goddard

The water shines, a pebble skips across the face
A dozen times, then disappears, not a trace left behind
"Mirror Man," The Human League

I try to be plain with readers and audiences that I am a "believing historian"—that I participate in many of the metaphysical movements and thought schools I write about. This is actually not an unusual thing for a historian, even though most do not announce it. Some of our key histories of the traditional faiths, as well as of new religions such as Mormonism and Christian Science, come from scholars who have commitments within those faiths. Rather than serve as a blinder, the vantage point of critical belief can be helpful, since it is almost impossible to understand a religious movement without out a personal sense of the values and practices that emanate from it.

In addition, I do not view esoteric or alternative spiritual expressions as schisms, set apart from the historic march of faith. Rather, many nontraditional spiritual movements provide novel means and new windows on the perennial aim of all contemplative religion: refinement of the individual, heightened perception of reality, and the leavening of coarse ideas and relationships into finer ones. Religion, in its true form, aims to elevate the self and restore man to his highest nature. I do not endeavor to place thought movements in museum cases for classification—rather, I believe that the seeker-historian must be able to identify workable, practical philosophies, which improve human conduct in the here and now. Thought systems that do not accomplish those ends should be discarded. Effectiveness is the currency of any ethical or spiritual program.

In my study of mystical systems and philosophies, the most impactful, elegant, simple, and dramatically challenging outlook I have personally come across emerges from twentieth-century spiritual philosopher Neville Goddard. I have referred to Neville, who went by his first name, at various points in this book. We will now consider his ideas—and how to use them—in a comprehensive manner. If you read this chapter with earnest interest, regardless of whether you follow Neville to the ultimate extent of his vision, your life and perceptions will not remain unchanged. You will, I am confident, look back, in either the long or short term, and agree with that statement.

Neville was born to an English family on the island of Barbados in 1905. He was one of ten children: nine boys and a girl. In 1922, at the age of seventeen—his youthful intrepidness marked a difference between his era and our own—Neville migrated to New York City to study theater. He had some success, appearing in roles on Broadway and in silent films (an entertainment columnist in 1926 hailed the young actor's "remarkable likeness to Rudolph Valentino"), and traveled internationally with a dance troupe. During his performing career, Neville came in contact with a wide range of mystical philosophies. By the early 1930s, the dancer and actor came to feel that he had discovered the master key to existence, namely that *the human imagination is God the Creator.*

The purpose of this chapter is to suggest, chin out, that the young man's discovery may have been right. You can vet that for yourself. I'm going to be very plain in giving you his spiritual system. I follow it with a consideration of Neville's personal history—where he came from, the gestation of his ideas, who he influenced—and why I believe that Neville was a vastly prescient thinker. In particular, I lay out some of Neville's techniques—he insisted that his ideas must be tested in the laboratory of experience—and explore, both here and in the next and final chapter, how they resound in unsensationalized considerations of developments in quantum physics, psychical research, and neuroscience. I'm also going to consider the intriguing teacher called Abdullah, whom Neville identified as a spiritual master who tutored him in New York City in the 1930s.

THREE STEPS TO TRUTH

Neville regarded his philosophy as the most important aspect of his life. Although he had dashing good looks and the savoir faire of a Cary Grant (with a mid-Atlantic accent to match), he rarely submitted to professional photographs or chased after publicity. He independently published ten books, spoke in rented auditoriums or churches, and had little visible media presence. The one major piece of journalism about him was a profile written during World War II in the *New Yorker,* not a magazine known for its mystical proclivities. In short, we know Neville's name strictly because of his ideas, and I want to start with them.

Neville believed, simply, that the God of Scripture is a metaphor for the human imagination. All of the stories from Scripture, in both the Old and New Testament, he taught, have no basis in history. The entire Bible is a book of Near-Eastern symbolism, written in a pictographic language that is intended to provide a blueprint for the individual's inner development. In Neville's interpretation, the New Testament symbolically tells of God descending into human form. Humanity falls asleep to its own Divine or Christ essence, with the individual—i.e., each one of us—believing himself or herself confined to a limited, coarse world of material parameters. Not yet fully developed, man is crucified in the agony of this forgetfulness—as Christ cries out on the cross, "My God, my God, why has thou forsaken me?"—only to be gloriously resurrected into the realization of his Divine nature. This potentiality exists within every individual, and this journey from sleep to awareness unfolds in every life, even if multiple recurrences are required for its fruition.

Neville concluded, based on his revelatory reading of Scripture, his probing as a philosopher, and his intimate experiments, that the illumined writers of Scripture never intended to communicate the existence of an exterior God outside the individual's own visualizing-imaginative faculty. The creative force traditionally called God exists solely within you, as your imagination, and is constantly out-picturing your mental images and emotively charged thoughts into reality. This is occurring all the time, as you think, plan, ponder, and fall in and out of emotive states, but you are asleep to it. The aware individual, Neville emphasized, can learn to conjoin his intellect and emotions into the consciously creative act.

Without this awareness, we suffer, we cry, we have fleeting joys, we fight—always believing that we are responding to stimuli rather than creating it. In what we call death, we eventually depart these physical forms, having passed through our existence in a state of slumber without understanding that what we call "I" is a form in which Creation is experiencing itself.

Coming to the realization that you, through your imagination, are a branch of the Creator, Neville taught, can bring you into the bloom of powers written about in metaphor in the New Testament and symbolized in the story of Christ resurrected. I must note that he meant all of this in the most literal sense. There was nothing inexact or qualified in Neville's thought. He took a jarringly radical stand and continually challenged his listeners: *try it.* Try it *tonight,* he insisted, and if it doesn't work, disregard me, disregard my philosophy. Prove me wrong.

Neville was not a businessman or a seller of spiritual products. He delivered his lectures Grateful Dead–style, in which he allowed any listener to freely record and distribute them (which is why hundreds of his talks now circulate online). Most of his books are in public domain due to nonrenewal of copyright. With Neville, there's nothing to join, no label to wear, and little or nothing to buy. There's just the man and his ideas—and your option to experiment with them.

The method behind Neville's ideas is reducible to a three-part formula. This formula is simple, but do not approach it lightly. It requires persistence. We will now explore each of the three steps.

1. Every creative act begins with a passionate desire.

Do not be fooled by how easy that sounds. We walk around all day with desires, thinking: I want this and that; I want money; I want sex and romance; I want this person to pay attention to me; I want this achievement; and so on. Yet much of the time, as we've seen, we have only superficial understandings of our desires. We're dishonest about what we truly want because we often don't want to acknowledge, in our innermost hearts, what we really wish for. We live in a society that is, on the surface, filled with personal license and freedom; but we don't like admitting to ourselves things that we feel are unfitting of a given image we've cultivated—a self-image designed to appeal to others, but that may no longer fit us. We also confuse *means* with *desires,* sometimes saying we want a certain job, for example, when what we really want is security.

I want to share a personal story, and I'm going to be very personal in this chapter because I'm describing in Neville a man and a philosophy that is enormously challenging—*and enormously practical,* if you take this material seriously—and I feel obligated to warranty my words with personal experience. Experience is the empiricism of the inner path, and I will start with one that bears upon this first step: *clarified desire.*

Years ago, I knew a woman who was a well-known psychic—not a household name but widely known. I felt she had an authentic psychical gift. I didn't like how she lived, because I personally felt that she could be a violent person; not physically violent but emotionally: she would manipulate people, bully them, and generally push them around.

I didn't particularly like her—but I did feel that she had a true intuitive gift. (People are often lopsided—the possession of keen insight into human affairs does not equate with ethics or empathy.) I was talking to her one night; we were having a conversation in a parking lot somewhere, and she stopped and said to me: "Do you know what you want? You want power. But your problem is, you have an overdeveloped superego."

As soon as I heard this I wanted to push it away. And I spent years pushing it away. I thought: "I don't want power like you. I don't want the power to push people around, to bully people, to be violent toward people." And I so recoiled from what she said. But it haunted me. I could never get away from it.

Sometimes we are (and must be) haunted by something unacknowledged within ourselves, something that makes us deeply uncomfortable—but that might be true.

I had to acknowledge, as years passed, that this flawed messenger did tell me the truth. But she also provided an example of the kind of power *I didn't want:* the power to manipulate and grab. She got me thinking about the power I did want: the ability to exert my will—physically, intellectually, and artistically—in order to see my plans through in the world. And to do so directly, with as few intermediaries as possible. To select relationships based on mutual affinity, respect, and constructiveness, or to forego having a relationship. To fulfill my true debts, but not empty obligations.

When Neville talks about desire, he's not speaking superficially. He really wants you to get down into the guts of matters, where you might want something that makes you uncomfortable. There are ways we don't like to see ourselves. But Neville maintains that desire is God speaking to us. And God *is* us. To walk away from a deep personal yearning is to walk away from God within yourself. In essence, we all want the same thing: to fulfill our essential inner ideals, to exercise, exhibit, and exert ourselves in the natural direction toward which we are always being pulled. And we want to be seen and understood.

I was once in a spiritual group where a woman described in a meeting how she had made an ice sculpture outside of her home on a bright winter day. Some friends came to visit in the afternoon, and she was anxious that they see her sculpture before it melted in the sun. She was embarrassed to direct her friends' attention to it, yet at the same time she was eager for her work to be seen. The woman recounted this as a kind of a confession, expressed with remorse over her presumed egotism. I honor the self-disclosure with which she told her story—yet I feel strongly that she had nothing to feel ashamed of, and nothing to confess. She created something beautiful. She had the ability to do so. Why shouldn't she want her friends to see it—why hide her light under a bushel? Her work made the world more beautiful before it was taken by the afternoon sun, and her act spoke of her to the world; which is to say it spoke of all human creativity.

Self-expression is to be honored. Creative acts are to be seen. Your clarified desire is the language of holiness; it is the urge toward creation. "And God saw that it was good." Be exquisitely clear, passionate, and forthright about your goals.

2. Your imagination is fertilized in a state of physical immobility.

This is where we start to *enact* our desires. Creativity begins when we purposefully enter a state of physical immobility. Choose a time of day when you would like to meditate. The time of day Neville chose was 3 p.m. He'd eat lunch, get tired, and willingly enter a sort of drowsy state, usually in an easy chair; though a sofa, bed, or yoga mat would work just as well. Now, this is very important because we often think of meditation as a state of keen awareness or mindfulness. We don't think of meditation as drowsiness. People use these terms in different ways. Neville believed, and I have referenced this before and will return to it, that we heighten our apparatus of mental creativity when we enter the "in between" state of hypnagogia. The hypnagogic state, you'll recall, is the stage between wakefulness and sleep. You're in it at night just as you're drifting off; you're in it in the morning just as you're coming to (sometimes called hypnopompia). At such times, our minds are deeply sensitive and impressionable.

I noted earlier that people who suffer from depression or grief often describe the early morning hours as the most difficult time of day. The reason, I'm convinced, is that our rational defenses are down. We are conscious and have sensory awareness; but we are also in a deeply suggestible, impressionable state, in which emotions are powerfully felt. We lack a sense of proportionality. I can attest from experience that if you are trying to solve a personal problem, never attempt it while lying in bed at 5 a.m. Do not. Get up and meditate, or watch television, or do whatever you must, but keep in mind that your logical apparatus is at its ebb, and the gremlins of the unconscious are liable to run amuck.

When your analytic mind is at a low point and your emotions are churning, it is a very difficult time to confront problems or attempt acts of perspective. But it is also, and for some of the same reasons, *a propitious time to visualize your desires.* With your rational barriers down, your mind, if properly harnessed, can take you in remarkable directions. As I've noted and will return to, psychical researchers have made the extraordinary finding, studied under strict conditions, that when subjects are induced into a state of relaxed hypnagogia, usually through comfortable sensory deprivation, the mind is found to possess heightened abilities of extraphysical communication.

Neville said to enter a state of physical immobility of this sort. You may find it easiest to do just before you go to sleep at night. He didn't say to do it in the morning, but I think we can extrapolate that that's a viable time, too. You can do it during a time that you set aside for meditating, as long as you're comfortable and undisturbed, and can uninhibitedly enter a very relaxed physical state. If you have difficulty relaxing, as many people do, allow the body to take over naturally by entering and becoming aware of this state before drifting off at night. You will, however, need to do the next step—step three—*before* falling asleep, because it requires a measure of conscious control over your thoughts.

3. Form a vivid, simple mental scene of your desire fulfilled.

A woman at one of Neville's Los Angeles lectures told him that she yearned to be married—what should she do? He told her to enact the feeling of a ring on her finger. Just that. Mentally assume the feeling of a ring on your finger, in a very simple way. Feel its weight, the density of the band, and maybe feel yourself spinning it around on your finger. Don't do anything physically, just feel it.

What you do want? Maybe you want something from another individual. Enact a scene that implies its fulfillment. Maybe just a handshake—something that communicates that you've received what you wanted, that it's done. *Do not see yourself doing this action as if you're watching it on a screen. You must feel yourself in the action and see it from the perspective of actually performing it. You're not watching, you're performing.* If I want to imagine myself climbing a ladder, Neville said, I do not see myself climbing a ladder—*I climb!*

Make your mental scene very basic; it keeps the mind from wandering. Identify one clear physical action that communicates the attainment of your goal *and then think and feel from that end.* Always think from the end of the goal fulfilled. Neville told people that when you open your eyes, you'll be back here, in the ordinary world, which you might not want to be in; but if you persist in this practice, your assumption will eventually harden into fact. If you want to be in Paris and you open your eyes and you're still in Queens, you may be disappointed. But keep doing it. An extraordinary event, he taught, will unfold to secure what you have pictured.

One point must be clarified—and this point must be stated more clearly throughout New Thought culture in general. Neville noted that the visual state must also be accompanied by an emotive state. The positive-thinking movement often errs in equating thoughts with emotions. They are entirely different. I have a physical existence, I have an intellectual existence, and I have an emotional existence. The reason we feel so torn apart is because these things are all going their own way. I say that I'm not going to eat something—well, the body wants to eat it, and next thing it's in my mouth. I resolve to be calm—but the emotions are furious, and I experience an outburst. I determine that I'm going to think, to use my intellect—but my passions are running off doing something else.

When you enact your mental picture of fulfillment, you must experience the emotions that you would feel in your state of achievement. This method may come naturally to some people, including those who are actors. Neville himself was an actor and performer. Anyone who has studied method acting learns to use an inner monologue to enter an emotional state. That's a useful exercise. Read Constantin Stanislavski's *An Actor Prepares*. You must get your emotions into play. Let's say you want a promotion at work. You might picture your boss shaking your hand and saying, "Congratulations, congratulations." You have to *feel* the emotions that would naturally be yours in that state. "Feeling is the secret," Neville wrote.

It is the mental state, and not physical effort, that creates. Some people ask whether this is a formula for passivity. I am friendly with a successful manufacturing executive in the Midwest. He is an avid student of Neville's ideas. He asked me a question one day: He feels confident in picturing an outcome. But his board of directors, he explained, demands details—they want to know: How will it get done? In following Neville's teachings, he feels that he's already doing all that is needed. And for years it has worked. But he must answer to people who aren't going to accept a metaphysical formula as a business plan. What should he do?

My response to him was to plan and act as the board requires—and continue to mentally create as before, remaining true to his conviction that that's where the real power resides. We live in a world of Caesar and must abide by material demands. My friend will lose the confidence of his board if he fails to act. We are called upon to perform in both worlds: the seen and the unseen. If Neville wanted to take a train somewhere, he didn't just sit in his room—he went out and purchased a ticket. We are surrounded by people living in outer life. Play the role that outer life requires. "Render unto Caesar." But remember the underground spring from which all creation arises.

There is one further aspect to the act of mental actualization: creative silence. Do not blurt out what you're attempting or act hastily to move things along. Ralph Waldo Emerson captured this principle in a passage from his journals of January 15, 1857: "This good which invites me now is visible & specific. I will at least embrace it this time by way of experiment, & if it is wrong certainly God can in some manner signify his will in future. Moreover I will guard against evil consequences resulting to others by the vigilance with which I conceal it." In other words, we risk no harm to ourselves and others in our acts of mental intention, provided we avoid rash outer action. Seen from Neville's perspective, this supplies the inner meaning of Christ's injunction to be "wise as serpents and harmless as doves." For example, let's say you harbor romantic feelings toward someone. To speak of it could cause embarrassment, rejection, or ruinous consequences. Do not speak. Allow your mind to act; if you are wrong (as you may be), you will eventually know by perception. And if you are correct, events will unfold harmoniously, as good events always do and must from God—your mind—who speaks in the Beatitudes of gentleness, love of neighbor, and generosity.

So to recap the formula: First, clarify a sincere and deeply felt desire. Second, enter a state of relaxed immobility, bordering on sleep. Third, enact a mental scene that contains the assumption and feeling of your wish fulfilled. Run the little drama over and over in your mind until you experience a sense of fulfillment. Then resume your life. Evidence of your achievement will unfold at the right moment in your outer experience.

EVIDENCE OF THINGS NOT SEEN

"If there is evidence for a thing," Neville said in 1967, "does it matter what the world thinks?" He considered experience the one true test of his method.

I want to tell a personal story along those lines. You have no reason to trust what I'm saying unless I can attest to it. Neville always urged listeners to test him, asking, with his beautiful clipped accent: "What do you most desire, right now? Go home this night and test it, and prove me wrong." He always issued a challenge. Here is a story from my acceptance of his challenge. It is one episode that I've experienced among others, but I offer it here because it's recent, explicit, and verifiably real.

In addition to being a writer, I've also been a publisher. Until recently, I worked at a division of Penguin Random House where I focused on New Age and metaphysical books. In 2012, I began searching for the rights holders of a 1936 self-help book that I wanted to republish: *Wake Up and Live!* by American writer Dorothea Brande. In her book, Brande argued that most mediocrity arises from a peculiar feature of human nature, which she called "a will to fail." In short, we are so terrified of humiliation that we sabotage our plans to avoid being tested. This self-sabotage takes the form of procrastination, excuses, missed deadlines, and apathy. Our fear of humiliation surpasses our hunger for success—and so, Brande argued, we avoid rather than strive. If, however, you could "act as if it were impossible to fail," you would bypass these self-defeating behaviors and come into new energies.*

I spent a year locating Brande's descendants in Vermont so I could license rights to this book. As I prepared the book for publication, I learned of an audio publisher who wanted to issue a narrated edition. I am passionately involved in audio narration, and I told this publisher of my eagerness to narrate it. I had successfully recorded two books previously for this publisher and expected a quick yes. But to my disappointment, the person would not get back to me. My emails and phone calls

---

*I agree with Brande's argument, but take a far dimmer view of her character today than when I first pursued her book. I later learned of her marriage to, and sympathies for, American fascist Seward Collins (1889–1952), who voiced support for Hitler. Although none of this is reflected in *Wake Up and Live!*, it is a grotesque and profoundly disappointing revelation.

went unreturned. I was brimming with passion and had a good track record with this publisher, but I just couldn't get anywhere. So, I went into Neville's three-part exercise, and I formed a mental picture. I'm not going to describe it because it is personal—but it was very simple.

While I was doing the exercise, the publisher finally did reply to me—and said no. Rather than submit to despair or confusion (though I felt some of both), I continued with my exercise. I had my mental picture, and I worked with it probably two or three times a day for about two weeks. Then, out of the blue, with no outer intervention on my part, my company's subsidiary rights manager called me and said: "Guess what? Someone else actually stepped in and bought the rights to that book. It's no longer with that other publisher; there's a new audio publisher."

I said, "Would you please tell that new audio publisher that I am eager to read this book?" She promised to. She got back to me very shortly and reported that the new publisher said: "I sent Horowitz an email a week ago, asking him to read a different book, but he never responded." I had gotten no such email. I went into my spam folder and found nothing there. I then went into a different, more stringent spam folder—and there was his message. It pertained to a different, unrelated book. However, he had written to say that he not only wanted me to read that other book, but he also wanted me to read a total of three books for him. I signed on to do three books—including *Wake Up and Live!*, which he had just acquired.

I went from being ignored, to being told no, to recording three books, including the one I desired, which had migrated from one publisher to another. I did nothing to influence these events in outer life. I'm a lousy Monday morning quarterback anyway, and I didn't try to call in a favor or make some maneuver. I did Neville's exercise. I went from a no, to then learning that the rights had moved to a new publisher, to hearing the new publisher say: "I contacted him a week ago, why didn't he get back to me?"

I've since done dozens of projects with that publisher, with whom I now work regularly. There are reasons it could be argued that this turn of events was completely ordinary. And I'm not oblivious to them. But I can say this: having been in publishing for more than two decades, long enough to have a sense of how things work, none of it *felt* ordinary.

"Take my challenge and put my words to the test," Neville said in 1948. "If the law does not work, its knowledge will not comfort you. And if it is not true, you must discard it. . . . I hope you will be bold enough to test me."

This is *your* test. It is exquisitely private. You don't have to declare fealty to anything. These ideas are purely a matter of inner exploration. Much of our culture has lost a sense of individual experiment. Let this be your sojourn to Walden. The highest freedom can be found in searching for and living from your own intimate sense of meaning. Go and experiment.

PORTRAIT OF THE MYSTIC

Since Neville exemplified his own philosophy, it is also important to understand something about him personally. Let's pick up where we began earlier: the island of Barbados, where Neville was born in 1905. He was not born into the wealthy, landowning class. Rather, he was part of a large, somewhat scrappy family of British merchants. They ran a small grocery and provisions business.

Transplanted from his tropical home to the streets of New York, Neville led a precarious financial life. The actor and dancer got by on jobs such as elevator operator and shipping clerk when theater work ran scarce. He did land some impressive roles, including on Broadway. But most of his stage work dried up with the onset of the Great Depression. Food was not a guarantee; he often wore the same suit of clothes and bounced around shared rooms, including on Manhattan's Upper West Side.

In 1955, a gossip column reported that Neville came from an "enormously wealthy" family who "owned a whole island" in the

Caribbean. This is invention—but over the course of time, the Goddard family did, indeed, become rich. This family of green grocers grew into Goddard Enterprises, which is today a large catering and food service that employs about 6,500 people in the Caribbean and Latin America. They cater events, and also prepare meals for airlines, oil rigs, factories, and other industrial facilities. Neville's father Joseph, called Joe, founded the business, and ran it with Neville's older brother Victor, of whom Neville spoke frequently in his lectures. Everything Neville described about the rise of his family's fortune matches business records and reportage in Caribbean newspapers. But there is a more dramatic example of Neville's descriptions conforming to fact.

In the years immediately before and after World War II, Neville lived in New York's Greenwich Village, a place that he relished. He resided with his wife and daughter at 32 Washington Square, a handsome, redbrick apartment building on the west side of Washington Square Park. (His prospering family had since put the actor-turned-mystic on a stipend.) Neville spent many happy years there. He was pulled away from home by the draft during World War II. He told a story in his lectures, however, of being quickly and honorably discharged from the Army and returned back home thanks to the methods I've been describing. This story interested me, and I decided to track it as best I could.

According to Army records, Neville was drafted on November 12, 1942, a little less than a year into America's entry into the war. This was the height of the war, when nearly every able-bodied male was being drafted. At age thirty-seven, Neville was a little old for the draft, but men were conscripted up to age forty-five. He wanted no part of the war, and longed to return home to Greenwich Village. At that time, he was newly married with a four-month-old small daughter, and he also had an eighteen-year-old son from a previous marriage. He had obligations that most draftees did not. While stationed for basic training at Camp Polk in Louisiana, he asked his commanding officer for a discharge—and was given an abrupt refusal. Neville decided to use his methods of mental creativity. Each night, as he described it, he would lie down on his army cot and before drifting to sleep would picture himself back in Greenwich Village. He would see from the perspective of being in his apartment with his wife and family, and walking around Washington Square Park. He continued, night after night, in this imaginal activity.

Finally, Neville said, seemingly out of nowhere, the commanding officer came to him and asked, "Do you still want to be discharged?" Neville said, "Yes, I do." And the CO said, "You're being honorably discharged." When I first read this in his lectures, I was suspicious. Why would the United States Army discharge a perfectly healthy, athletic male—Neville was lithe and fit as a dancer—at the height of the war effort? It made no sense.

So, I found Neville's surviving military records. He was, as noted, inducted in November of 1942. I spoke to an Army public affairs officer who also confirmed that Neville was, as he told it, honorably discharged within five months in March 1943, which was the date of his final Army pay stub. The reason, as recorded by the military, is that Neville was "discharged from service to accept employment in an essential wartime industry."

I asked the public affairs officer: "This man was a metaphysical lecturer—how is that a vital civilian occupation?" He replied: "Unfortunately Mr. Goddard's records were destroyed in the 1973 fire at the National Personnel Records Center," about a year after Neville's death.

The *New Yorker* of September 11, 1943, ran an extensive profile of Neville—this confirmed his being back on the lecture circuit at that time. He is depicted speaking all around town, in midtown at the Actor's Chapel, downtown in Greenwich Village, in full swing of his "employment in an essential wartime industry." I cannot say precisely what happened; I can only report that the logistics, as he described them, were accurate. I have found similar validation of several of his claims: he describes an unlikely story, says he used his method, and the unexpected occurs. I've reviewed his census records, citizenship application, military records, and other documents that track his whereabouts and employment and can only say that his timelines and workday details match up.

METAPHYSICAL LINEAGE

I want to consider where Neville's ideas came from, or rather their point of embarkation—because Neville was in no way a derivative thinker. I have come across phrasing in his early writing that suggests influences from French mind theorist Émile Coué and American psychical researcher Thomson Jay Hudson, whose 1893 book *The Law of Psychic Phenomena* was influential in the late nineteenth and early twentieth centuries. Hudson attempted to demonstrate that mediumistic phenomena resulted from natural laws of clairvoyance rather than spirits or the supernatural.

Although Neville took his ideas in a bracingly original direction, the basics of his system were New Thought, which rejects materialism as the foundation of life and sees reality based primarily in spiritual rather than physical laws. Modern positive-mind philosophy is a distinctly American phenomenon and is very much a homegrown thought school, the roots of which are traceable to the Transcendentalist culture of New England in the mid-nineteenth century and the mental-healing movement that grew in its wake.

Those are the modern points of reference. But when tracking the history of ideas, one learns (or ought to) that virtually every thought in currency has been encountered and articulated in varying ways at diffuse points of history. Ideas about the causative nature of thought appear in the Greek-Egyptian philosophy called Hermeticism, which flourished in the city of Alexandria in the decades immediately following the death of Christ. Writers in the Hermetic tradition captured centuries of Egypt's oral history and symbolism, recording it in Greek.

They believed they were transmitting the ideas of a mythical demigod who the Greeks called Hermes Trismegistus, or thrice-greatest Hermes, who was a Hellenized version of the Egyptian god of writing and intellect, Thoth.

One of the key ideas in Hermetic philosophy is that through proper preparation, including diet, meditation, and prayer, the individual is permeated by divine forces and gains higher powers of mind. This teaching reemerged during the Renaissance when translators and religious scholars rediscovered the Hermetic writings. In the Renaissance mind, Hermes was a figure of great antiquity, of the same vintage as Moses.

Renaissance thinkers had hoped that in finding Hermetic literature, some of which had been stowed away in monasteries during the Dark Ages, they had unearthed works of the greatest antiquity, which described a primeval theology predating Judeo-Christian culture. The Hermetic literature was later correctly dated to late antiquity, following the death of Christ. When this timeline was readjusted, the ideas of Hermeticism began to fall out of vogue. Renaissance intellects had pinned great hopes on the antiquity of the Hermetic writings; and when those writings were redated, many of the same philosophers and scribes, their hopes of antiquity dashed, drew the conclusion, tragically for the Western intellect, that the entire project of Hermetic literature was compromised. Hence, to this day, there are few good translations of the Hermetic literature. It has been neglected. But what Renaissance (and later) thinkers failed to grasp was that even though the Hermetic writings themselves were not very antique, they nonetheless captured a worldview that had existed in oral tradition for an extraordinarily long time. A primeval philosophy is, in fact, present, at least in part, in the Hermetic manuscripts, which postdate the ideas found in them. This is the ancient antecedent to Neville.

Some Hermetic ideas and concepts about the divinity of the mind reentered Western culture through the influence of individual philosophers and artists, including British poet and mystic William Blake

(1757–1827). Blake's thought made a direct impact on Neville. Blake believed that our limited perceptions imprison us in a fortress of illusions. But the one True Mind, the great Creative Imagination, or God, can permeate us. "If the doors of perception were cleansed," Blake wrote, "every thing would appear to man as it is, Infinite." In states of higher sensitivity, the visionary poet reasoned, we can feel the effects of this Great Mind coursing through us.

Neville was also influenced, as I noted earlier, by Émile Coué, the self-trained French hypnotherapist. Coué died in 1926, but shortly before his death he lectured on two tours to the United States. Coué was, for a time, hugely popular in the United States and Europe. It was Coué who first spread the idea of using the drowsy, hypnagogic state for mental reconditioning. Another of Coué's ideas that figured into Neville's thought—you can find the language in Neville's 1945 book *Prayer: The Art of Believing*—is that each of us contains two competing forces: *will* and *imagination*. The will is our self-determinative and decision-making apparatus. The imagination is the mental pictures that govern us, particularly with regard to self-image and emotional judgments we hold about ourselves and others. Coué said that when will and imagination are in conflict, the imagination invariably wins. The emotional state always overcomes the intellect.

As an example, Coué said, place a wooden plank on the floor and ask someone to walk across it. He will have no problem. But if you raise that same wooden plank twenty feet from the ground, the subject will likely be petrified, even though there is no difference in the physical act. He is capable of crossing the plank; the risk of falling is minimal. But the change in conditions makes him *imagine* falling; this fosters an emotional state of nervousness (which also makes him more accident-prone). Coué reasoned that we must cultivate new self-images—but we *cannot* do so through the intellect. We must do so by suggesting new ideas to ourselves while in the subtle hypnagogic state. He called his method "auto-suggestion." It was essentially self-hypnosis. I find some hint of that in Neville—though he far surpassed it.

The purpose of human existence, Neville taught, is not to recondition your imagination, but be *reborn* from within your imagination. You experience your imagination—your true self—as physically lodged in your skull, which functions as a kind of womb. Neville, in the culmination of his mystical vision, believed that you must be reborn from within your skull, and that you will have that actual physical experience, maybe in the form of a dream, but nonetheless a vivid, tactile experience of actual rebirth from the base of your skull. You will know in that moment that you are fulfilling your central purpose.

Neville described this vividly. He had the experience himself in New York City in 1959. He told of the tangibly real dream of being reborn from his skull. Minerva was said to be reborn from the skull of Zeus or Jupiter. Christ was crucified at Golgotha, the place of the skull. You and I, Neville said, will be reborn from within our skulls. Later in Neville's career, a speaking agent warned him to stop emphasizing this kind of esoteric material in his talks—he had to return to more familiar themes, like the fortune-building powers of the mind, or he would lose his audience. "Then I'll tell it to the bare walls," Neville replied. Although he drew smaller crowds, Neville continued to speak of this mystical rebirth for the rest of his career, until his death in Los Angeles in 1972.

RESURRECTION

Neville was not widely known when he died, but his popularity has risen in recent years. His books have probably sold more copies over the past decade than they did throughout his lifetime. He was always a kind of underground name, but he influenced a wide range of cultural figures. One of them was All-Star pitcher Barry Zito, who first exposed me to Neville. When I interviewed Barry in 2003, he said to me, "You must really be into Neville." I had never heard of him. Barry was incredulous. I immediately got a copy of Neville's 1966 book

Resurrection, which many name as their favorite. I was hooked. That conversation was, in a way, a turning point in my life. It also played a part in Neville's revival. In February 2005, I published a historical profile of Neville in *Science of Mind,* which later appeared as the introduction to a popular anthology of his writing, spurring renewed interest in the mystic, and helping me on my path as a historian of alternative spirituality.

The New Age writer Wayne Dyer borrowed a lot from Neville in one of his final books, *Wishes Fulfilled,* in 2012. But another, more compelling writer also received an influence from Neville: Carlos Castaneda, of whom I'm a greater admirer. Castaneda famously told tales of his tutelage under a mysterious instructor, a Native American sorcerer named Don Juan. (My admiration for Castaneda may seem misplaced given what I wrote in the first chapter about the need for verity in spiritual nonfiction. I plead guilty to an inconsistency; his distillation of wisdom attains a sublimity that surpasses whatever devices he uses to convey it.) Neville probably influenced the mystical chronicler through accounts of his own intriguing teacher, Abdullah. As it happened, Castaneda discovered Neville's work in the mid-1950s through an early love interest in Los Angeles, Margaret Runyan, who was among Neville's most dedicated students. Margaret met Castaneda when he was an art student at UCLA—she wooed him by slipping Carlos a slender Neville volume called *The Search,* in which she had inscribed her name and phone number. The two became lovers, and later husband and wife.

Runyan spoke frequently to Castaneda about Neville, but he responded with little more than polite interest—with one exception. In her memoirs, Runyan recalled Castaneda growing fascinated when the conversation turned to Neville's discipleship under an exotic tutor:

It was more than the message that attracted Carlos, it was Neville himself. He was so mysterious. Nobody was really sure who he was or where he had come from. There were vague references to Barbados in the West Indies and his being the son of an ultra-rich plantation family, but nobody knew for sure. They couldn't even be sure about this Abdullah business, his Indian teacher, who was always *way back there* in the jungle, or someplace. The only thing you really knew was that Neville was here and that he might be back next week, but then again . . .

"There was," she concluded, "a certain power in that position, an appealing kind of freedom in the lack of past and Carlos knew it."

Neville frequently told the story of his teacher Abdullah, whom he described as a turbaned black man of Jewish descent. Starting in 1931, he said, Abdullah tutored him in kabbalah, Scripture, number symbolism, and mind metaphysics. He depicted Abdullah as a somewhat taciturn, mysterious man whom he met one day at a metaphysical lecture in New York in 1931. He walked in and Abdullah told him, "Neville, you are six months late!" Neville recalled, "I had never seen this man before." But the turbaned figure insisted, "The brothers told me you were coming, and you're six months late."

The storyline of hidden spiritual masters like Abdullah has a long pedigree in the alternative spiritual culture. Nineteenth-century Russian occultist and transplanted New Yorker Madame H. P. Blavatsky, and her collaborator Colonel Henry Steel Olcott, popularized the concept. Olcott, a retired Civil War colonel, founded the original Miracle Club in 1875, and later that year formed the influential Theosophical Society, of which the short-lived, earlier group was a precursor.

Olcott and Blavatsky claimed that their hidden teachers sent them mysteriously timed letters, which gave direction, succor, and guidance. One of their teachers, Olcott said, instructed Blavatsky and him to relocate to India in 1878. Once there, the pair helped instigate the Indian independence movement; Gandhi named himself an admirer. Olcott delivered speeches on Buddhism throughout India, Sri Lanka, and Japan, and through his tours and opening of religious schools, ignited a Buddhist revival in the East. Blavatsky and Olcott were enormously effective, in their way, and attributed their impact to the guidance of unseen masters.

For his part, Neville said that he experienced his first true awakening while under mentorship to Abdullah in the winter of 1933. The dancer ached to get out of Manhattan to spend Christmas back home with his family in Barbados. But he had no money for travel. Abdullah told him: "Walk the streets of Manhattan as if you are there, and you shall be." Neville walked the streets of the Upper West Side, adopting the feeling that he was on the palm-lined lanes of Barbados. He would return to Abdullah and complain that it wasn't working. The teacher would slam the door in his face and say, "You're not here, you're in Barbados!"

As Neville told it, one day before the last ship sailed from New York to his West Indies home, he received a letter from his long-out-of-touch brother Victor, who, without any outer antecedent or intercession on Neville's part, sent him fifty dollars and a first-class steamer ticket to Barbados for the winter. Neville was transformed by the experience; he practiced Abdullah's teaching of mental assumption ever after.

FELLOW SEEKERS

I want to mention a few other figures that did not know Neville personally but had some intersection with his way of thought. One is British occultist Aleister Crowley, whose former secretary Israel Regardie knew and wrote about Neville in New York the 1940s.

Crowley made a very interesting statement in his *The Book of the Law,* which he handwrote through what we might call channeled perception in 1904; he published it in several limited venues before issuing the first generally available edition in 1938. In his introduction to *The Book of the Law,* Crowley wrote:

Each of us has thus an universe of his own, but it is the same universe for each one as soon as it includes all possible experience.

This implies the extension of consciousness to include all other consciousnesses.

In our present stage, the object that you see is never the same as the one that I see; we infer that it is the same because your experience tallies with mine on so many points that the actual differences of our observation are negligible. . . . Yet all the time neither of us can know anything . . . at all beyond the total impression made on our respective minds.

Neville said something similar in 1948: "Do you realize that no two people live in the same world? We may be together now in this room, but we will go home tonight and close our doors on entirely different worlds. Tomorrow we will go to work where we will meet others, but each one of us lives in our own mental and physical world."

Neville meant this in the most literal manner. He believed that every individual is a universe unto himself. And everyone who you experience, including me as I write these words, is rooted in you, as you are ultimately rooted in God. We exist in a world of infinite possibilities and realities. And when we mentally picture something, we're not creating it—it already exists; we're simply selecting it. The very fact of being able to experience something mentally confirms, in this world of infinite mind, that your imagination is the ultimate arbiter. Everything that you can picture already *is*, and our concurrent realities crisscross one another's as dreams that morph, fade, and blend, one into another.

Part of Neville's perspective also figures into psychical research. A contemporary of Neville's, but not an acquaintance, was psychical researcher J. B. Rhine. Beginning in the early 1930s, Rhine, as noted, performed tens of thousands of trials at Duke University to test for clairvoyant perception. He experimented on subjects with a five-suit deck called Zener cards. Using these cards, a subject had a one-in-five—

or 20 percent—chance of correctly guessing an image, such as a cross, circle, or square. Across thousands of carefully controlled trials, Rhine documented that certain individuals averaged above a 20 percent hit rate, inclusive of negative sets. (Years later there was some controversy that Rhine didn't count negative results. This kind of omission was common among academic researchers, including Rhine, in the 1930s; his lab was among the first to correct this practice, so that Rhine's data ultimately reflects the full results. Moreover, the chance probability of his results are so astronomically low that even hypothetical unreported data would fail to offset it.)

Hit rates were not always dramatically higher than 20 percent—in authentic psychical research a deviation can be subtle but consistent. If someone, over the course of thousands of trials, continues scoring, say, 25 percent, 26 percent, 27 percent, beyond all rates of chance, and the results are parsed and juried to ensure against corruption—Rhine's data was subjected to greater scrutiny than the most rigorous pharmaceutical trials*—you then have evidence of some kind of anomalous transfer of information in a laboratory setting.

Rhine was a demure figure. He had a quiet way of relegating what could be a monumental observation to a footnote. Rhine remarked that higher-than-average hit rates on Zener cards usually correlated with a subject who experienced feelings of enthusiasm, positive expectancy, a belief in the possibility of ESP, and a generally encouraging testing environment. By contrast, when boredom or fatigue set in, results tended to drop. When a subject's interests were revived, results would again spike. Our culture hasn't begun to deal with the implications of Rhine's experiments. But the suggestion, as with placebo trials,

---

*This was a phenomenon Rhine recognized—and embraced. In his reply of March 15, 1960, to Warren Weaver, he wrote: "Even though the methodology and standards of evidence may compare favorably with other advances of natural science, they have to be superior in parapsychology because of its novelty; and conceivably, too, by making them still better, everything may be gained in overcoming the natural resistance involved."

is that *positive expectancy correlates favorably with extraphysicality,* at least among subjects for whom ESP exists as a potentiality.

I consider parapsychologist Charles Honorton as Rhine's immediate successor, even though the two men had tensions between them. In the 1970s, Honorton began a series of ESP trials called the ganzfeld experiments, which we considered in chapter 4. Honorton and his collaborators theorized that if you could induce a subject into a near-sleep state—we're speaking once more of hypnagogia—it might be possible to heighten some kind of clairvoyant faculty.

Honorton's tests typically involved two participants. One subject, the "receiver," would be placed into a state of comfortable sensory deprivation, fitted with eye coverings and white-noise headphones, and seated or reclined in an isolation tank. The other subject, the "sender," would be seated in a different room, where he would attempt to mentally convey an image, such as a flower, rock, or boat, to the receiver.

In one version of the experiment, researchers used four images, of which three were decoys. In this case, the average guess rate was one in four, or 25 percent. In meta-analyses across thousands of trials, Honorton found results demonstrating a higher than 25 percent hit rate among subjects placed in the hypnogogic state.

Remember, you enter this state all the time: when you're napping, when you're dozing off at your desk, when you're going to sleep at night, when you're waking in the morning. Neville's message was: *use it.* Do not be passive when entering this sensitive state but exercise gentle control and picture a goal. Honorton's experiments demonstrated heightened mental transference during hypnagogia, or at least statistics reflecting as much. He tested only one aspect of the ganzfeld affect. His experiments were tragically cut short in 1992, when he died at age forty-six (he had suffered lifelong health problems). Hypnagogia and its possibilities remain largely uncharted territory.

Another burgeoning field that intersects with Neville, and one more widely accepted than psychical research, is neuroplasticity. In short, neuroscientists can demonstrate through brain imaging that repeat thoughts alter the pathways through which electrical impulses travel in our brains. These findings have been used to treat obsessive-compulsive disorder (OCD).

UCLA research psychiatrist Jeffrey Schwartz has devised a protocol to treat OCD by encouraging patients in the very moment they experience an intrusive thought to *substitute* something in its place. The displacing thought or activity must be in the form of something compelling, whether pleasurable physical activity, listening to music, jogging, or anything you want, so long as it moves you off that obsessive thought. He has found that if you maintain this exercise, biologic changes manifest in the brain, altering the neural pathways associated with compulsion. Hence, we're seeing thoughts themselves change brain biology. This is a tantalizing piece of physical evidence for the kind of thought causation spoken of by Neville and other mind theorists.

What we're seeing hinted at in all these experiments, and others that I explore in the next and final chapter, is the expression of Neville's core thesis: You radiate and interact with the world around you by the intensity of your imagination and feelings. Yet our experience of time beats so slowly that we do not always notice the relationship between the world and our inner nature. You and I can contemplate a desire and become it, Neville wrote; but due to the slowness of time, it is easy to forget what we formerly set out to worship or destroy. Our perceptions and memory retention are so inexact, and our experience of time so slow, that we lose a sense of cause and effect.

How do we as individuals deal with this predicament—with this obfuscating shadow between perception and event? One way is to continually hone your perceptual abilities by exercise and observation of the material discussed in this chapter. In that vein, I want to leave you with a principle from American occultist P. B. Randolph, who lived in New York City in the mid-to-late-nineteenth century. Randolph was a man of African American descent and a tremendously original thinker and mystical experimenter. He died at the young age of forty-nine in 1875. His personal slogan was: "TRY." That's all: TRY. You'll recognize that from my preamble "Purpose" in the letter received by the founder of the original Miracle Club, Colonel Henry Steel Olcott (it arrived about two months before Randolph's death). This was Neville's principle, too. His challenge to the individual remains as ultimate as it is simple: put my ideas to the test, prove them to yourself, or dismiss them. What a tragedy it would be not to try. Have we lost the hunger for personal experimentation?

Poet William Blake, one of Neville's key inspirations later in life, wrote about the coarse nature of our slumbering perceptions. He sometimes described the human state in matters of geography and landscape. When Blake said England, he didn't mean the nation exactly, he meant the limited world in which we find ourselves. Our physical parameters are so deeply felt that we don't detect what's really going on. When Blake wrote about Jerusalem, by contrast, he meant true reality, which is revealed when the divine imagination of the Creator courses through sensitive men and women. Try to read these lines from Blake's 1810 ode, popularly called "Jerusalem," in the way that Neville experienced them:

> *And did those feet in ancient time,*
> *Walk upon Englands mountains green:*
> *And was the holy Lamb of God,*
> *On Englands pleasant pastures seen!*

> *And did the Countenance Divine,*
> *Shine forth upon our clouded hills?*
> *And was Jerusalem builded here,*
> *Among these dark Satanic Mills?*

Bring me my Bow of burning gold;
Bring me my Arrows of desire:
Bring me my Spear: O clouds unfold!
Bring me my Chariot of fire!

I will not cease from Mental Fight,
Nor shall my Sword sleep in my hand:
Till we have built Jerusalem,
In Englands green & pleasant Land.

CHAPTER ELEVEN

WHY IT WORKS

Toward a Theory of Affirmative Thought

Earlier I wrote about the relationship between ESP researcher J. B. Rhine and the influential scientist Warren Weaver. Weaver took a critical but supportive interest in Rhine's work. However, Weaver issued a warning to Rhine. Speaking as both a scientist and a grant-making executive, he told the parapsychologist after a visit to his lab in 1960, that, regardless of how extensive a body of statistical data Rhine amassed, and however carefully that data was vetted to safeguard against pollution, the scientific community would not accept his findings unless he reached a theory of how ESP worked. He had to provide a model of the mechanics of thought transmission.

It was clear that extrasensory transmission couldn't be explained through the "mental radio" model, since, according to Rhine's tests and those of others, it was unaffected by time, distance, or physical barriers. Since extraphysical sensation seemed to violate generally acknowledged laws of mechanics, what was happening? Rhine never did arrive at a precise theory of *how* mentality exceeded the apparent boundaries of sensory transmission. He acknowledged to Weaver, "There is now an increasingly candid recognition of the difficulty as an essentially metaphysical one. Psi phenomena appear to challenge the assumption of a physicalistic universe."*

I cannot sidestep this kind of question with respect to positive-mind mechanics. If thought possesses causative properties, as I've been arguing, then what are its means of transaction? Late nineteenth- and early twentieth-century New Thought writers who endeavored to explain the mechanism of thought causation—the last time this question was seriously considered in the field—would at a certain point, lean on theological terms without adequate definition or justification. I cannot do that in the twenty-first century, when we've seen too many things that, in past centuries, were considered "spiritual," including healing itself, which are today explainable in demonstrably physical terms.

So, what *is* going on when thoughts appear to make things happen?

I believe it has something to do with the nature of time and the illusion of linearity. What we typically call time, referring to events past, present, and future, is simply a mental construct used to organize our lives—e.g., this happened yesterday, that may happen tomorrow. What is really happening is that we select—not manifest but select—from an infinite variety of things that are occurring all at once, all around us. When our illusion of order is pierced by an emotive, focused thought, we experience what might be called a "time collapse," in which events, perceptions, and notions of past, present, and future all blend together. We then see the world as it really is: whole and not subdivided into points on an imaginary line, extending from birth to death.

I am now going to offer three pieces of personal testimony, which seem to suggest the permeability of time and events. Following these testimonies, I will compare what was experienced with developments in quantum physics, which suggest a macro explanation for events like those I describe. These events, remarkable as they are, will, I suspect, remind you of things that you've experienced more than once in your own life.

---

*Rhine was referring to commonly accepted mechanical laws at the time. For psychical researchers in the twenty-first century, studies in quantum theory, retrocausality, extra-dimensionality, and other areas suggest a set of physical laws that surpass the known, and that may serve as a kind of "macroverse" within which ordinary mechanics function.

Time Collapse One: The Hospital

At age twelve I was hospitalized for an unnamed emotional disorder. What do you call it when a young adolescent just won't go to school? No one quite knew. I didn't know. Home and school life were a terrible torment in a new neighborhood where we couldn't afford to live. We hid our middle-class poverty behind used clothes, a Volkswagen Beetle with a concealed hole in the floor, and the rationing of household goods from toilet paper to mustard. If your last name is Horowitz and you're from Long Island, people assume you're well off. They have no clue.

In sorrow, and amid the torment of school bullies, bizarre teachers, and generalized daily fear, I reacted by refusing to attend school. (In retrospect it was not an entirely dysfunctional approach.) In a set of circumstances that are uncommon today, my mother's secretarial job was a unionized position. As a result, we had comprehensive medical insurance. And insurance companies, at that time, actually paid claims rather than harassed legitimate claimants into retreat and disengagement. So, the family shrink decided, probably wisely, that I should be sent to a place known euphemistically as the "adolescent ward" at North Shore University Hospital, where I had been born a dozen years earlier.

The adolescent ward was a psychiatric unit for teens (I was among the youngest) who were drug addicted, suicidal, depressed, or had some unnamed but chronic problem. One of the kids there was a mentally challenged fifteen-year-old named Ned who had been kicked out of other facilities for behavior violations. He had virtually no schooling. My roommate Tommy was a fifteen-year-old track star who had, during an acid trip, pushed his mother through a plate-glass window. One night, two girls snuck off the locked ward and were later arrested driving drunk in a stolen car, going the wrong way on a one-way street.

And yet, for all this, it was a kind of happy place. We would listen to Jimi Hendrix and endlessly scheme ways to sneak in pot, or at least get high off sniffing the glue that nurses innocently allowed me to keep for my plastic models. On most days, the biggest problem on the adolescent ward was how to relieve boredom. One time we marked up the walls with graffiti, which I had to clean myself when I wouldn't rat out my collaborators (perhaps in misplaced zeal to honor my rabbi's admonition against trash talk). Meals, TV, and card games took on a restless routine. To mix things up, the nurses occasionally showed movies in the evenings on a wall in the common area. This was the predigital era: there were no DVDs, and even videotape was fairly rare, used for school documentaries but not feature films. If you wanted to show a movie, you had to use a 16-millimeter print on a film projector. There weren't many big-ticket movies available to us this way.

One night, they screened (or rather walled) a light comedy in which Cary Grant played a boozy, misanthropic Allied spy stationed on a remote Pacific island during World War II. The eccentric enjoyed his isolation and occasionally radioed his handlers about Japanese planes he spied overhead. One day his tropic idle was upended when he found himself forced to shelter a stranded French schoolmistress and her gaggle of schoolgirls. The unshaven American and prim French schoolmarm butt heads, fight like dog and cat, and then— almost needless to say—fall in love. It wasn't exactly *Taxi Driver,* but it was what we could find. I never caught the name of the movie and even as I write these words, almost forty years later, I do not know it.*

These events occurred in 1978, when I was twelve. More than twenty years later, the evening before my marriage, on April 7, 2000, I had the unexpected occasion to return to North Shore University Hospital. My mother had recently divorced her second husband, David Weinberg, a gruff, razor-smart Queens tax accountant. (In full bloom of adolescent obnoxiousness, I once asked him whether the national accounting chain H&R Block was "better" than him. "Of course they're better!" he replied sardonically. "I'm just some schnook in a basement in Queens.") David was alone—his two sons were en route from California—and hospitalized with complications from Parkinson's disease. He was too sick to attend the wedding or our rehearsal dinner that night, and I wanted to go see him before we left the country on our honeymoon. We had fought, but were close.

When I entered his room I was shocked: his condition had severely deteriorated. Although his mental faculties were strong (which he demonstrated

---

*I discovered recently that the film is *Father Goose,* Grant's penultimate screen role in 1964.

to his doctors by reciting his medications in backward alphabetical order), his arms and legs were emaciated, as thin as pencils, like the limbs of a concentration camp victim.

He put up a brave front, and introduced his roommate in the next bed. "Say hello to Vince," he told me. I glanced over to say hi and noticed that Vince was watching a hospital television mounted by a metal bolt to the wall. I looked at the TV—on the screen was the same Cary Grant movie from twenty-two years earlier. A place where my life began and where, at age twelve, it seemed to end, or at least stall, was now somewhere I was returning on one of the most joyous nights of my life, my wedding eve, to visit another man whose life was ending (David died during our honeymoon), and to reencounter an obscure movie from decades earlier, whose name I did not even know. (Cary Grant, I later realized, played an island-dwelling eccentric like my idol Neville; I had even compared the two men in other contexts.)

This was the experience of a time collapse. There was no past, present, or future. It felt, indelibly, that everything was occurring at once. The emotions, the setting, the triumph, the failure, the beginning, the ending—none were bound by time. All was *now*.

Time Collapse Two: The Monkees

In the summer of 2016, for no reason that I can consciously identify, I starting getting into the TV band The Monkees. Although I had watched *The Monkees* reruns as a kid, I had no particular attachment to them. As a teen (and today) my musical tastes ran to The Who, The Clash, and the Dead Kennedys. But I developed a conviction that The Monkees were more than just a made-for-TV package. I came to feel that the ensemble surpassed its manufactured image, and that the group's music—they did eventually play their own instruments and write their own songs—was more than just jingly pop rock. (And, mind you, jingly pop rock is also more than it seems: The Monkees' most recognizable hits came from song writers including Carole King and Boyce and Hart.)

In the grip of Monkeemania, and possessed of non-sequitur zeal, I began listening to The Monkees all the time. My kids got to know their hits like "I'm Not Your Steppin' Stone" and "Last Train to Clarksville"—and my wife wondered where in the world this late-blooming interest came from. I began to recall past events in my life that involved The Monkees. Comrades of mine in a socialist youth group had written a hilarious send-up of "Steppin' Stone" to satirize activists who postured lefter-than-thou: "I knew you when you were a Young Republican / Now you're struttin' 'round like you're Ho Chi Minh."

In summer 2016, I wrote about The Monkees in my book *The Miracle of a Definite Chief Aim*. I held up the band as an example of how financial success can serve an artist. In 1967, The Monkees had sold so many millions of records that they gained sufficient commercial clout to compel their handlers and producers to allow them to write and play their own music.

I continued to pursue this interest in The Monkees into the fall of that year. At that time, the *Washington Post* asked me to review a new biography of Norman Vincent Peale, author of *The Power of Positive Thinking*. I eagerly accepted. (This is the event I recounted in chapter 4 where I wrote of anticipating a significant assignment.) It was a good experience, and I thought to myself that I would like to write more for the *Post*. The day that the Peale review ran, I heard from another editor there: Did I know, he asked, that Mike Nesmith of The Monkees was into Christian Science? No. Would I like to review Nesmith's new memoir, *Infinite Tuesday*? Yes, definitely. Did I know or have any connection to Nesmith? No. But—how weird it was: for months previously, with no foreknowledge, I had been immersing myself in The Monkees' music and background. This episode had the feeling of another time collapse. I wrote the following in my review, exactly as I experienced it:

> Nesmith's finest moments in *Infinite Tuesday* are when he offers his own sprightly metaphysics: "One continuously positive idea I've carried from my early years is an ever-expanding notion that the past does not create the present—that what seems set in perpetuity can be instantly changed. This was never an argument for randomness, but more of a sense of an eternal present that was constantly updating, revealing more and more of the moments that comprised infinite Life."
>
> He is right: reality doesn't travel straight lines. Months before being asked to review Nesmith's book, with no awareness of its publication or any

correlation, I developed a renewed attachment to the Monkees. My kids got to know their lyrics. My wife scratched her head at this sudden fancy. Is there some connection? I have no idea. But within that doubt, Nesmith would agree, lies Infinite Tuesday—a nonlinear realm to which he is a distinctly likable, erudite guide.

Time Collapse Three: The Magic Staff

I do not often write down dreams. I seldom recall them for more than a few minutes after waking and, frankly, I sometimes think dreams are little more than a psychological retread of the day's events, a potpourri of impressions, and a working through of anxieties. But one that I did record, in a rare act, on July 30, 2014, and later forgot all about, came back to me with a shock. Here is exactly how I wrote it down in a little red book by my nightstand:

> Dreamt I was speaking (at A.R.E.?*) to 2 auditoriums—one "New Age" & one like a movie theatre. Joked about it. Both melded into one neat, tidy room following a distraction in the New Age auditorium. I carried a cane— wondered how the audience took it. Did they like it?

For reasons that I cannot recall, I also added below this recollection: "Reading July 15, 1928." This referred to one of A.R.E. founder Edgar Cayce's channeled readings, in which he stated: "the spiritual is the LIFE; the mental is the BUILDER; the physical is the RESULT."

Having no recollection of this dream, and forgetting I had written it down, I visited A.R.E. almost two years later, on April 1, 2016, to deliver a talk on Cayce's positive-mind philosophy. During my visit, I received a tour of the Cayce archives, which holds in its collection a walking stick—or cane— belonging to nineteenth-century medium Andrew Jackson Davis, who coined the term Law of Attraction and also popularized séances and Spiritualism. Next to Cayce, Davis is the most influential medium in American history. The archive was rightly proud of owning Davis's walking stick, which had

---

*A.R.E. is the Association for Research and Enlightenment, the spiritual growth center founded by early twentieth-century mystic and psychic Edgar Cayce in Virginia Beach, Virginia, where it continues to operate today.

figured prominently into his personal mythos, as well as the title of his 1857 autobiography, *The Magic Staff.*

In his account, Davis recalls a transforming event that occurred on a winter night in 1844 in the Hudson Valley surroundings of his hometown of Poughkeepsie, New York. That night, as Davis tells it, he had fallen into a very deep trance state—he was experimenting with mesmeric trances*—and had difficulty returning to ordinary consciousness. He stumbled back to his rented room. Collapsing on the bed of his third-floor bedroom, Davis entered a deep sleep. He recalled being awakened by a voice—it was his dead mother, urging him to come outside. The bearded youth rushed downstairs and out onto Main Street where he encountered a vision of a flock of unruly sheep being herded by a shepherd who seemed to need his help. The vision vanished in a "rosy light" and Davis, his mind illuminated and his body light, embarked on a psychical "flight through space," which took him across the frozen landscape of the Catskill Mountains. Whether his journey was psychical or physical wasn't entirely clear, though it may have been both, as he vanished until the following day.

Davis's night journey culminated inside the stone walls of a small country graveyard set deep in the woods. There, he said, he met the spirit of the legendary mystic-scientist Emanuel Swedenborg. The Swedish seer told the boy: "By thee a new light will appear." Davis also received what he termed a "Magic Staff," which first seemed physical but he later understood was mental in nature. Later an astral message revealed to him the true nature of the staff's magic: "Behold! Here is Thy Magic Staff: UNDER ALL CIRCUMSTANCES KEEP AN EVEN MIND. Take it, Try it, Walk with it. Believe on it. FOR EVER."

A few days after I returned home to New York from Virginia Beach, I happened upon the written record of the forgotten dream, made two years earlier. I came across the red notebook while I was clearing out some items from a nightstand drawer. The dream was of my being at A.R.E., of trying out my ideas in both

---

*I am referring to the trance states popularized by Viennese occult healer Franz Anton Mesmer (1734–1815), whose work prefigured hypnotism, mental healing, and the earliest studies of the subconscious mind. Mesmer was a seminal figure in the development of modern transcendental culture. I consider his career in *One Simple Idea.*

a New Age and mainstream setting, and of carrying a cane. Here are pictures of me holding Davis's staff in the A.R.E. archive, taken by archivist Laura Hoff:

The Magic Staff: Mitch with Andrew Jackson Davis's walking stick in the archives of the Edgar Cayce Foundation, Virginia Beach.

"A. J. Davis": The seer's initials etched in the handle of his walking stick.

As it happened, the Cayce reading that I had appended to my dream ("the mental is the BUILDER") had formed the basis for my April 2016 talk.* As mentioned, I do not often have foresightful dreams, and I had no memory of this one. Yet the dream encapsulated, and in some ways foresaw, every major theme of my current professional life: my search to combine intellectual seriousness with positive-mind metaphysics; my endeavor to harmonize my work as both a historian and seeker (I call myself a "believing historian"); my attempts to determine how I relate to mystical figures whom I admire and critique, such as Davis and Cayce; and, finally, my working through of my own style of writing and presenting in the two worlds, New Age and mainstream, which I simultaneously occupy, just as I occupied two types of auditoriums in the dream. Discovering Davis's staff in the archive that day was like encountering a milestone or marker, which suggested to me that I was progressing, if fitfully, along the right lines. To find the staff felt portentous enough. You can detect the emotions on my face in the photographs. But to rediscover my overlooked dream, and to realize that I had mentally lived out that scene some two years earlier, brought me a stirring sense of time collapse, in which events were playing out in a nonlinear manner.

---

*This talk is adapted in my 2017 book *Mind as Builder: The Positive-Mind Metaphysics of Edgar Cayce.*

☀

I also had another dream, more recent to this writing, in which a phrase came to me: "Expectation follows." In that dream, I attributed the phrase to David Lynch, whose movies disrupt the linearity of time. *Expectation follows.* What does it mean? I think it suggests that we can reach backward in time and rearrange events from the past in conformity with expectations in the present. The immensely important twentieth-century spiritual teacher G. I. Gurdjieff taught: the past controls the future but the present controls the past.

Time is not what we think it is.

MULTIPLE WORLDS

I am limiting myself to the three examples above; there are other time-collapse episodes, and I am sure most readers could add a list of their own. Critics can call these things coincidences or willful stretches to locate meaning in randomness or claim that they are not as statistically offbeat as they may appear. I observed earlier that, although statistics are wonderful for measuring odds and possibilities, the one thing they cannot measure is the depth of emotional investment or gravity an individual feels in connection with event. The alignments, for example, that led to my seeing the Cary Grant movie again in the hospital—my childhood experience there, visiting a man on his deathbed, it being the eve of my wedding—carried a degree of poignancy that no actuarial table can quite get at. In such instances, we really don't know what's going on. People venture theories that make them feel a sense of security or portentousness: to the logician, it's simple chance; to the New Ager, it's the "universe" revealing something; to the psychical researcher, it's precognition.

All of these things may have varying degrees of truth depending on the circumstances. But something else may also be at work—and this relates to the ever-tense subject of quantum physics. Thoughtful people sometimes roll their eyes at the mention of quantum physics, bracing themselves for a woo-woo alert. I myself have cautioned New Agers against cherry-picking concepts from this complex field in order to but-tress personal beliefs. But, the fact is, there really is room for a conver-sation between physicists and mature students of metaphysics. We just have to be measured—and patient—on both sides. If we can do that, the payoff may be remarkable in terms of a deepened question about the nature of time and the formation of events.

For the last several years, a thickening stream of New Age books and documentaries have attempted to use quantum theory to "prove" that the mind possesses causative powers. Enthusiasts say that quan-tum experiments demonstrate that an observer's presence or perspective determines the nature of objects on a subatomic scale. Some clinicians theorize that everything we experience may stem from conscious percep-tion. Robert Lanza, chief scientific officer of the Astellas Institute for Regenerative Medicine and adjunct professor at Wake Forest University School of Medicine, has argued that death itself is ultimately a mental phenomenon—we "die" because the mind perceives demise.

Physicists are rightly vexed when concepts in quantum theory get quoted or picked over in sensationalistic ways. Many scientists want to slam shut the door on the (admittedly dim) popular connection between quantum physics and the theorized reality-shaping properties of the mind. But ongoing findings in quantum physics—when consid-ered without half-baked understanding or exaggeration—keep pushing that door back open.

Let's start with the basics before linking all this together with my time collapse proposition. Many physics journals today discuss what is called the "quantum measurement problem." In essence, more than eighty years of laboratory experiments show that atomic-scale particles appear in a given place only when a measurement is made. Astonishing as it sounds—and physicists themselves have debated the data for generations—quantum theory holds that no measurement means no precise and localized object, on the atomic level.

Put differently, a subatomic particle literally occupies an infinite number of places (a state called "superposition") until observation manifests it in one place. In quantum mechanics, a decision to look or not look actually determines what will be there. In this sense, an observer's consciousness determines objective reality in the subatomic field.

Some physicists would dispute that characterization. Critics sometimes argue that certain particles are too small to measure; hence any attempt at measurement inevitably affects what is seen. But there exists a whole class of "interaction-free measurement" quantum experiments that don't involve detectors at all. Such experiments have repeatedly shown through interference patterns that a subatomic object literally exists in more than one place at once until a measurement determines its final resting place.

How can this be demonstrated? In the parlance of quantum physics, an atomic-scale particle is said to exist in a wave state, which means that the location of the particle in space-time is known only probabilistically; it has no properties in this state, just potentialities. When particles or waves—typically in the form of a beam of photons or electrons—are directed or aimed at a target system, such as a double-slit, scientists have found that their pattern or path will actually change, or "collapse," depending upon the presence or measurement choices of an observer. Hence, a wave pattern will shift, or collapse, into a particle pattern. Contrary to all reason, quantum theory holds that opposing outcomes simultaneously exist.

The situation gets even stranger when dealing with the thought experiment called "Schrodinger's cat"—and this touches directly on the nature of time and reality. The twentieth-century physicist Erwin Schrodinger was frustrated with the evident absurdity of quantum theory, which showed objects simultaneously appearing in more than one place at a time. Such an outlook, he felt, violated all commonly observed physical laws. In 1935, Schrodinger sought to highlight this predicament through a purposely absurdist thought experiment, through which he intended to force quantum physicists to follow their data to its ultimate degree.

Schrodinger reasoned that quantum data dictates that a sentient being, such as a cat, can be simultaneously alive and dead. A variant of the Schrodinger's cat experiment could be put this way: Let's say a cat is placed into one of a pair of boxes. Along with the cat is what Schrodinger called a "diabolical device." The device, if exposed to an atom, releases a deadly poison. An observer then fires an atom at the boxes. The observer subsequently uses some form of measurement to check on which box the atom is in: the empty one, or the one with the cat and the poisoning device. When the observer goes to check, the wave function of the atom—i.e., the state in which it exists in both boxes—collapses into a particle function—i.e., the state in which it is localized to one box. Once the observer takes his measurement, convention says that the cat will be discovered to be dead or alive. But Schrodinger reasoned that quantum physics describes an outcome in which the cat is *both* dead and alive. This is because the atom, in its wave function, was, at one time, in either box, and either outcome is real.

Of course, all lived experience tells us that if the atom went into the empty box, the cat is alive; and if it went into the box with the cat and the poisoning device, the cat is dead. But Schrodinger, aiming to highlight the frustrations of quantum theory, argued that if the observations of quantum-mechanics experiments were right, you would have to allow for each outcome.

To take matters even further, a cohort of quantum physicists in the 1950s theorized that if an observer waited some length of time, say, eight hours, before checking on the dead-alive cat, he would discover one cat that was dead for eight hours and another that was alive for eight hours. In this line of reasoning, conscious observation effectively manifested the localized atom, the dead cat, the living cat—*and also manifested the past,* i.e., created a history for both a dead cat and a living one (the living one might be hungry, restless, etc.). Both outcomes are real.

Decades of quantum experiments make this model—in which a creature can be dead/alive—into an impossible reality: an unbelievable yet entirely tenable, even necessary, state of nature. Schrodinger's thought experiment forced a consideration of the meaning of quantum mechanics, though not many physicists pay attention to the radical implications.

So, why is there an apparent divide in our view of reality, in which one set of rules governs the events of the micro world and another set governs the visible world in which we live? It may be due to the limits of our observation in the visible world. Some twenty-first-century quantum physicists call this phenomenon "information leakage."

The theory of information leakage holds that the apparent impossibilities of quantum activity exist all around us. They govern reality. However, when we step away from whatever instrument we are using to measure micro particles and begin looking at things in larger frames and forms, we see less and less of what is really going on. We experience a "leakage" of data. William James alluded to this dynamic in his 1902 Gifford Lectures, which became *The Varieties of Religious Experience:* "We learn most about a thing when we view it under a microscope, as it were, or in its most exaggerated form. This is as true of religious phenomena as of any other kind of fact."

Only future experiments will determine the broader implications of particle phenomena in the visible world in which we live. For now, however, decades of quantum data make it defensible to conclude that observation done on the subatomic scale (1) shapes the nature of outcomes, (2) determines the presence or absence of a localized object, and (3) possibly devises multiple pasts and presents. This last point is sometimes called the "many-worlds interpretation," in the words of physicist Hugh Everett. This theory of many worlds raises the prospect of an infinite number of realities and states of being, each depending upon our choices.

The flexibility of time and the possibilities of many worlds are not so far out when considering that Einstein's theories of light speed and time, which have now been proven, demonstrate that time *does* slow down as a physical fact for an entity moving near or at light speed. This is called "time dilation." Light speed outstrips the horizon of time. Some physicists have further theorized the existence of "tachyons," particles that surpass light speed. If an object *surpasses* light speed, it moves along a time continuum so immeasurably fast that it can be said to occupy all points at once. The object has effectively obtained omnipresence.

The nonlinear nature of time is also suggested in experiments outside of quantum physics. Recall the EEG experiments of researcher Dean Radin from chapter 4. In those experiments (among others), Dean and his collaborators at IONS found that under certain conditions vital signs in the brain, skin, and heart demonstrate a sentiment of stimuli (such as light, sound, or touch) *before those stimuli actually get delivered.* Dean and his colleagues reported on their EEG experiments in a 2011 paper in the journal *Explore,** noting that "the common sense notion of a unidirectional flow of time might be a façade, an approximation of a deeper reality in which both past and future influence the present."

This also raises the question of whether the present can influence the past—of whether linearity is an illusion, and *cause and effect runs in all directions.* Time may be less like a straight line than a rotating, infinitely dimensional wheel, spinning out past-present-future as one symbiotic system. We experience linearity only when we view life as an isolated fragment or snapshot.

And here we encounter the frustrating but resilient thesis of positive thinking, which is that our thoughts, in some greater or lesser measure, determine our experience. Perhaps a better way of looking at it is that our thoughts select among infinite, nonlinear experiences, like a matrix grid that isolates a moment in space-time, and, hence, determines that as reality, as the seemingly sole outcome, experience, or memory.

If our thoughts and feeling states can be understood as sensory devices, then they can be said to *measure* things and inform our experience. Everett's concept of multiple worlds and outcomes could be the

---

*"Electrocortical Activity Prior to Unpredictable Stimuli in Meditators and Non-Meditators" by Dean I. Radin, Ph.D., Cassandra Vieten, Ph.D., Leena Michel, and Arnaud Delorme, Ph.D., *Explore* 7, no. 5 (September/October 2011).

key to why thoughts are causative, or, put differently, *why reality bends to the vantage point of the observer.* It's not so much that our thinking and perspective make things happen, but that we choose from among things that already exist in potential—like the superposition of a particle in a wave state. If thoughts register data, then a shift in the use of the sensory tool of thought—like a physicist deciding whether to take a measurement and the perspective from which it is taken—determines or alters what data is experienced. Based upon how your thoughts and feeling states are *used,* they expose you to different, and coexisting, phenomena.

This outlook finds its closest mystical analog in the ideas of Neville, who reasoned that the individual, through his feeling states and mental pictures, selects among infinite realities and outcomes. Of course, most quantum physicists wouldn't be caught dead/alive as Schrodinger's cat dealing with the theories of Neville. But there is an elegant intersection of possibility between his theology and the quantum theorizing of Schrodinger and Everett. This trifecta presents the most compelling explanation I know for the extraphysical impact of a sustained and directed thought.

Neville argued that everything you see and experience, including others, is the product of your own individual dream of reality. Through a combination of emotional conviction and mental images, he taught, you imagine your world into being—and all people and events are rooted in you, as you are ultimately rooted in God, or an Over-Mind. When you awaken to your true self, Neville argued, you will know yourself to be a slumbering branch of the Creator clothed in human form and at the helm of infinite possibilities. We all have this experience within our own dreams of reality.

I think we face greater barriers to this realization than Neville surmised. For one thing, we are, at times, so incapacitated by our psychological and emotional limitations that we cannot harness or experiment with the mind's higher mechanics. Hence, we must—and can—pray for salve in the traditional sense in order to feel sufficient morale and faith to exercise the agencies of thought. Here you may consider me at risk of doing what I've criticized in nineteenth-century mind-power writers: relying on theological references—and that is true. My best efforts to theorize unseen laws do not, in the end, disabuse me of a notion of the ineffable, to which one can make a prayerful or petitionary appeal.

What's more, I am not sure that we can, in this conscious existence, experience the personal surpassing of physicality in any but the most extraordinary moments. The cures recorded by Ainslie Meares did not erase the cycle of life and death. "Ye shall die as princes." Although nature is infinite and ever expansive—a fact experienced by the mind, which is, in a way, an organ of the ineffable—we, as branches of the Higher, may not, in these bodies, know infinite renewal.

USING IT

Neville made this observation in 1948: "Scientists will one day explain why there is a serial universe. But in practice, how you use this serial universe to change the future is more important."

How should one use it? Well, changing the past is the means to changing the future—and we change, or reselect, the past from our vantage point in what we perceive as *now*, the present. We've all attempted to fantasize about advice that we would give to our younger selves. We've asked or heard the question: "What would you do differently if you could go back to your childhood?"

Frankly, I'm not sure that I would do *anything* differently. It's not that I don't have regrets, or don't harbor memories that I would like to reverse. I harbor lots of pain and *what ifs?* But each one of these is, for all of us, a building block. To change or abrogate suffering might mean losing what we most cherish today, including vital traits that we developed in response. It might mean erasing what has driven us toward self-refinement.

What's more, we might discover ourselves *unable* to change, even if we possessed the hindsight of the present. We are not necessarily

Ebenezer Scrooge who can alter things based on consequences when visited by the Ghost of Christmas Yet to Come. In Luke 16, a condemned rich man is denied his request that a messenger of God be sent to warn his brothers about damnation: "If they do not hear Moses and the Prophets," God tells him, "neither will they be convinced even if someone rises from the dead." Compulsions, passions, and barriers of psychology—all the traits of human nature rued in our religious parables and classical myths—may prove greater than our perspective. If information alone altered behavior, there would be no addictions or automatisms. The twentieth-century mathematician and spiritual seeker P. D. Ouspensky considered this haunting theme in his time-travel novel, *The Strange Life of Ivan Osokin*.

Yet still—it *is* difficult not to wonder at the prospect of improving yourself in hindsight. We are not entirely without devices. Ethics and perspective do have a part in what happens in the present—we do have "Moses and the Prophets." So, why not expand our idea of what is possible in all realms of time, including the past? Let me put it this way: What if you *had* to go back in time? What if you had no choice? What if you discovered that, based on the nature of the mind, you were already doing it constantly? *Then* what would you do to live differently? Again, advice is often forgotten and neglected. So do not overplay the fantasy that merely *telling* yourself something spurs development or averts tragedy. But let's say you at least had the opportunity to healthfully or compassionately *shock* your younger self with a perspective of such indelible truth that it would engender a reordering of priorities, which may be the sole way that self-change actually occurs. William James called it a "conversion experience."

I attempted such an experiment. Recent to writing these words, I discovered an insight that I wanted to share with a younger me. As I was reading back over a journal entry that I had made at age fifty, I was astonished to discover how similar it was to the kinds of things I had written when I was in sixth grade. I was struck that all of my yearnings, all of my secret hungers and beliefs, all of my frustrations, traveled along the same path from early adolescence to middle age: the wish for power. (You'll recall the psychic I told you about in the last chapter.) Not the cheap power of manipulating others or telling them what to do; but rather the personal power to make my way through life with agency, with progression toward purpose and expression, and with assignation with those people and events that meet my ideals. All of my pathologies stemmed from one thing: frustration of this wish.

Now stop. Empty yourself of things that you've heard. And prepare yourself for this point. I was not missing the "higher purpose" of life. You are not missing it. This is the purpose: *The enactment of personal means.* It is the deepest yearning at the heart of our lives. Self-agency exists as a sacred yearning, always pressing at you, asking to be allowed to grow. If you deny it, you are denying the vitality of your existence. And if you deny it, *you will fail;* you will waste years "searching for God" or attempting to be "nonattached," without realizing that your earnest, nonviolent efforts toward self-expression and development *are the direction in which the sacred exists.*

As I said, I decided to try an experiment: Right now, from within my perception of my current circumstances, and from within the starkness of this realization, I determined to conceive and focus on what I would tell—and what I have told—my younger self, and live with the consequences. Here is what I wrote down:

- Immediately disassociate from destructive people and forces, if not physically then ethically—and watch for the moment when you can do so physically.
- Use every means to improve your mental acuity. Every sacrifice of empty leisure or escapism for study, industry, and growth is a fee paid to personal freedom.
- Train the body. Grow physically strong. Reduce consumption. You will be strengthened throughout your being.
- Seek *no one's* approval through humor, servility, or theatrics. Be alone if necessary. But do not compromise with low company.

- At the earliest possible point, learn meditation (i.e., Transcendental Meditation), yoga, and martial arts (select good teachers).

- Go your own way—literally. Walk/bike and don't ride the bus or in a car, except when necessary. Do so in all weather: rain, snow, etc. Be independent physically and you will be independent in other ways.

- Learn-study-rehearse. Pursue excellence. Or else leave something alone. Go to the limit in something or do not approach it.

- Starve yourself of the compulsion to derive your sense of well-being from your perception of what others think of you. Do this as an alcoholic avoids a drink or an addict a needle. It will be agonizing at first, since you may have no other perception of self; but this, finally, is the sole means of experiencing Self.

Does this kind of advice, practicable at any time of life, really alter or reselect the perceived past, and, with it, the future? I intend to find out. You must enact such a program and make that determination for yourself. *Expectation follows*. Now go and build.

THE MIRACLE CLUB

An Invitation to You

"Where two or three gather in my name I am there with them."

I've called this book the resurrection of the original Miracle Club. At certain points, I have also referenced 3 p.m. EST as a time of prayer. Here is where the two come together. I invite you to join me at that time every day, or whenever you like, for a few moments of silent prayer to affirm your ethical wishes and intentions. Barring a medical crisis or some emergency, I promise you that I will be with you in prayer every day at this time.

Christian tradition holds that 3 p.m. is when Christ died on the cross. A popular Catholic devotion calls it "The Hour of Great Mercy." It is a moment when people everywhere (varying by differences in time zone) pause in prayer, silent unity, and good intentions. This time is used not only for personal wishes but also for wishing others well, perhaps praying for someone's recovery from illness—anything that is needed in your life or that of another.

I set a permanent alarm on my phone for 3 p.m. EST each day and suggest you do the same. No matter where you are—on an elevator, in a meeting, even driving (as long as you don't take your eyes off the road)—you can pause from your onrush of thoughts to express gratitude and think on things that are of good report. We can do this together at 3 p.m. EST, or you can do it on your own or with others in your time zone.

Earlier, I defined a miracle as a circumstance or event that surpasses all conventional or natural expectation. Let all of us, in whatever situation and wherever we find ourselves, unite at this hour as a "miracle club" of prayer and good intentions.

Do not conform to the pattern of this world, but be transformed by the renewing of your mind. —Romans 12:2

CREDITS AND ACKNOWLEDGMENTS

I began writing this book in April 2016 on a trip to Sicily to visit my wife's family. The slower pace and saner lifestyle there gave me unexpected time to write—and made me very grateful, in more ways than I can say, to my wife, Allison Orr, to our sons Caleb and Toby, and to family members who gave me encouragement.

Personal thanks to journalist and historian Harvey Bishop for opening his blog to me (HarvBishop.com), where I wrote earlier versions of the chapters *The Ethic of Getting Rich, Working Class Mystic,* and *Why the Critics Are Wrong.*

Thanks to Dean Radin of the Institute of Noetic Sciences (IONS) for his guidance on questions of psychical research and quantum physics, and for generously sharing his insights and experiences.

Thanks to Stacy Horn, Sally Rhine Feather, and John Palmer for sharing resources on ESP research and helping me think through several issues. Stacy's book *Unbelievable* is, in my view, the finest thing written on J. B. Rhine.

Thanks to Heather Brennan for transcribing a talk I delivered on Neville in 2013 at the Brooklyn arts space Observatory, and my 2016 radio interview with David Lynch, both of which contributed to this book.

Thanks to my agent Amy Hughes, who "got it" from the start, and to Jon Graham of Inner Traditions for his immediate support of the book. Thanks, too, to Jennie Marx of Inner Traditions for her friendly and adroit handling of production.

Special thanks, as always, to my friend and colleague Joel Fotinos, who first exposed me to many of the ideas in this book.

ABOUT
THE AUTHOR

Mitch Horowitz was raised in a world of Bigfoot stories, UFO sightings, and Carlos Castaneda books. He grew determined to find the truth behind it all—and today Mitch is a PEN Award–winning historian and the author of books including *Occult America; One Simple Idea: How Positive Thinking Reshaped Modern Life; Mind as Builder: The Positive-Mind Metaphysics of Edgar Cayce;* and *The Miracle of a Definite Chief Aim.* Mitch has written on everything from the war on witches to the secret life of Ronald Reagan for the *New York Times,* the *Wall Street Journal, Salon,* and *Politico.* The *Washington Post* says Mitch "treats esoteric ideas and movements with an even-handed intellectual studiousness that is too often lost in today's raised-voice discussions." He is the voice of popular audio books including *Alcoholics Anonymous* and *Raven: The Untold Story of the Rev. Jim Jones and His People.* Visit him at MitchHorowitz.com and @MitchHorowitz.

INDEX